For Turner
Happy Birthday
May 11, 1994
John

# THE ILLUSTRATED HISTORY OF THE

# CIVIL WAR

RICHARD HUMBLE

# THE ILLUSTRATED HISTORY OF THE
# CIVIL WAR

RICHARD HUMBLE

COURAGE BOOKS

An imprint of
RUNNING PRESS
Philadelphia, Pennsylvania

# Contents

Text/compilation copyright © 1991 Multimedia Books Limited

All rights reserved under the Pan-American and International Copyright conventions.

This book may not be reproduced in whole or in part in any form or by any means, electronic or mechanical, including photocopying, recording, or by any information storage and retrieval system now known or hereafter invented, without written permission from the publisher and copyright holder.

Canadian representatives: General Publishing Co., Ltd., 30 Lesmill Road, Don Mills, Ontario M3B 2T6.

10 9 8 7 6 5 4 3 2 1

Digit on the right indicates the number of this printing.

Library of Congress Catalog Card Number 90–85262
ISBN 0–89471–995–5

Editors: Jeff Groman, Susie Ward and Andie Oppenheimer
Production: Hugh Allan
Design: Matthew Ward and Jack Wood
Picture Research: Tessa Paul

This book was devised and produced by Multimedia Books Limited, 32–34 Gordon House Road, London NW5 1LP.

Printed in Italy by New Interlitho

Published by Courage Books, an imprint of Running Press Book Publishers, 125 South Twenty-second Street, Philadelphia, Pennsylvania 19103.

# 1  The Union is Dissolved: 1859-1860

# ❛Citizens of the Slave-holding States of the United States! . . .

You have loved the Union, in whose service your great statesmen have labored and your great soldiers have fought and conquered . . . You have long lingered in hope over the shattered remains of a broken Constitution. Compromise after compromise, formed by your concessions, has been trampled underfoot by your Northern confederates. All fraternity of feeling between the North and the South is lost, or has been converted into hate; and we, of the South, are at last driven together by the stern destiny which controls the existence of nations . . . All we demand of other peoples is to be left alone, to work out our own high destinies. United together, we must be the most independent as we are the most important of the nations of the world . . . We ask you to join us in forming a Confederacy of Slave-holding States.❜

IF ANY SINGLE DOCUMENT is the birth certificate of the American Civil War, this stirring appeal is perhaps one of the best candidates. It was issued by the state convention of South Carolina on December 24, 1860—the same convention which, four days earlier, had announced South Carolina's secession from the United States of America and her birth as an independent nation. South Carolina's ringing invitation was accepted promptly, even joyfully, by the most fiercely independent slave states of the South and, within months, ten other states had followed suit and seceded from the Union. The Confederacy was a reality—with its own Constitution, President, and Cabinet—and the first shots of the American Civil War had been fired.

But why? What dark forces prompted a prospering and successful nation to cut itself in two and suicidally hurl one half against the other in what was up to then the costliest and bloodiest war in history? The American Civil War would last for four years, cost 600,000 American lives, destroy untold billions in property, pit brother against brother, and inflict an intractable sectionalism on American politics which was to last into our own time. It was four years of carnage, pitiless hand-to-hand combat, and massed slaughter on a scale the world had never known; and yet, when it was over and the butchery had finally come to an end, no more would be demanded of the losers than their bond not to fight against the United States again. Then they were permitted to go home, unmolested, and in most cases to take their horses and sidearms with them. A war of unparalleled viciousness had been settled by a peace of unparalleled magnanimity.

Once again, why?

## The Causes of the War

The simplest answer is that there is no simple answer. The causes of the American Civil War were many and complex and spread out over half a century. Indeed, there were probably as many causes of the war as there were men who marched off to fight it. Each man joined for his own individual reasons. He fought for dreams conscious and unconscious; for motives spoken and unspoken; for practical reasons; for economic reasons; he fought for high-minded abstractions with long Latin names; but just as certainly he also fought for reasons no more compelling than the prospect of a good scrap.

One thing, though, is clear. Popular mythology aside,

LEFT: Picking time. Slave women and children toil in the snowy fields of a cotton plantation under the overseer's eye. Custom-built for the fierce defense of slavery in the states where it flourished, cotton required only the crudest routine labor. And its low growth made it easy for overseers to supervise the slaves at work.

the American Civil War was *not* fought as an impassioned crusade against slavery. Slavery was important, of course, the one irreconcilable issue that could not be compromised or bartered away. In the end, slavery became the visible symbol of the cultural, geographic, political, and economic differences dividing North and South. As a symbol, it was to exert a disproportionate leverage on the emotions of men, but was not in itself the reason the two sides plunged into war. Without slavery, men of conscience on both sides would probably have found a way to settle their differences; with slavery, the war became in Seward's oft-quoted words, an "irrepressible conflict."

The two cultures which had evolved on either side of the Mason-Dixon line were united by a common history, a common language, and a more or less common heritage; but as they grew up, they grew apart—separated by differing values, philosophies, and institutions. Certain of these differences had been implicit in the two cultures from the moment of their arrival in the New World. Up until the time of the Revolution, remember, the Colonies were *English* colonies, peopled mainly by

*The American Constitution, drawn up in September 1787 "to form a more perfect Union, establish justice, insure domestic tranquillity, provide for the common defence, promote the general welfare, and secure the Blessing of Liberty to ourselves and our Posterity" — but at no stage to tackle the question of negro slavery, which was left like a time bomb for the future to defuze or explode.*

**An Ordinance,**

To dissolve the Union between the State of South Carolina and other States united with her under the compact entitled, "The Constitution of the United States of America."

We, the People of the State of South Carolina, in Convention assembled, do declare and ordain, and it is hereby declared and ordained,

That the Ordinance adopted by us in Convention, on the twenty-third day of May, in the year of our Lord one thousand seven hundred and eighty-eight, whereby the Constitution of the United States of America was ratified, and also, all Acts and parts of Acts of the General Assembly of this State, ratifying amendments of the said Constitution, are hereby repealed; and that the union now subsisting between South Carolina and other States, under the name of "The United States of America," is hereby dissolved.

EVANS & COGSWELL, PRINTERS, CHARLESTON.

*LEFT: South Carolina's Ordinance of Secession shows the state's palmetto flag, hoisted in defiance of the Stars and Stripes on December 20, 1860. This first act of secession formally renounced the allegiance to the Federal Constitution pledged by South Carolina in May 1788.*

*BELOW: Exultant headline in Charleston, proclaiming South Carolina's Ordinance of Secession on December 20, 1860. Observers noted that there was just as much jubilation over Lincoln's victory in the "fire-eating" states of the South as in the North. Those who believed that the South must follow its own destiny rejoiced that the hour had struck.*

THE

# UNION

## IS

# DISSOLVED!

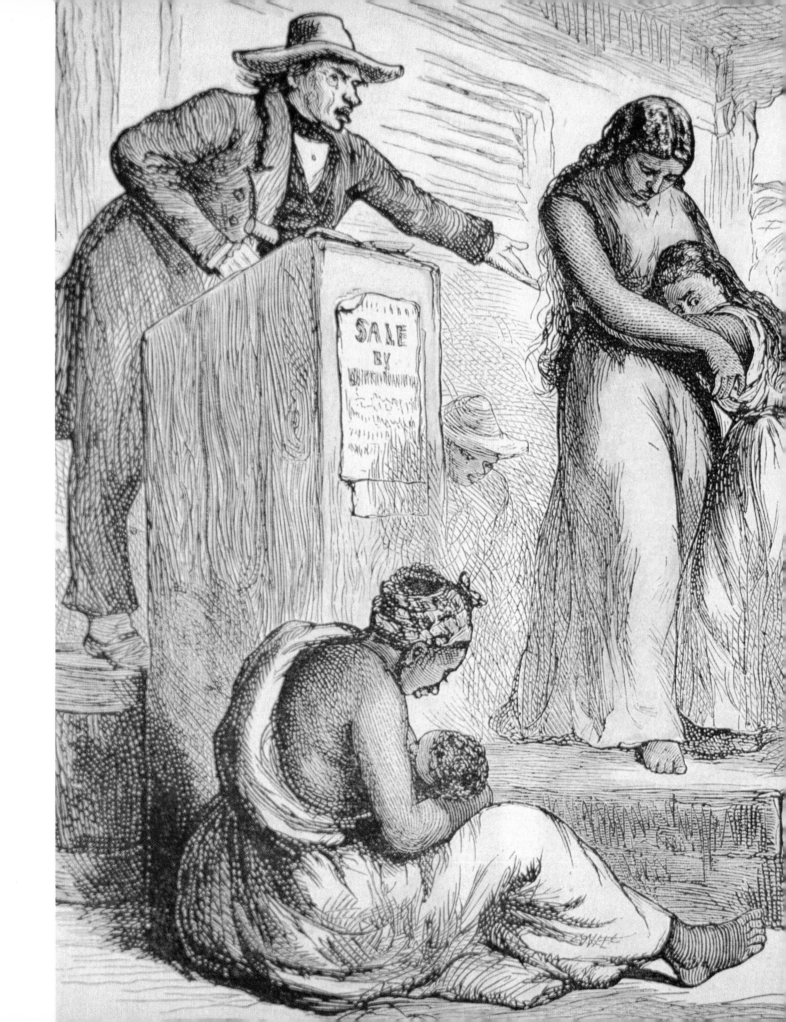

*The slave's worst nightmare come true: a mother and child on the auctioneer's block, for sale to different bidders. There was a constant market for attractive slave children "sold down the river" to the fashionable households — and brothels — of New Orleans.*

Englishmen or the descendants of Englishmen; to explain the differences between them, one does not have to look further than the English Civil War.

**North vs. South**

Northern society, as it spread outward from Plymouth Rock, came to represent mainly Puritan values: thrift, piety, hard work, self-reliance, and—as the descendants of nonconformists—the unspoken assumption that change was a positive quality in society rather than a negative one. On the whole, Northern society tended to be austere and sober, concerned with practical matters as much as with moral and religious issues. It valued men of reflection and ideas—theorists and writers—which may explain why the North, and New England in particular, developed a flourishing literary tradition. Above all, it valued achievers. At the top of Northern society was a plutocracy which rose or fell on its own abilities and hard work; at the bottom was a mass of "free labor," which was becoming increasingly concentrated into the large cities. There was also a broad-based middle class—business and professional people, and independent small farmers—who formed an educated and demanding electorate which expected their leaders to be responsive to their needs.

By contrast, the society which grew from the settlements along the James River inherited values more in keeping with the Cavalier tradition—a more genteel society, with elegant refinements and manners, altogether more gentlemanly and with a deeply conservative antipathy to change. This romantic spirit was seen in the Southerner's enjoyment of ease and pleasure; his love of field sports; his elaborate codes of manners, kinship, and hospitality; his touchy sense of honor settled all too often with pistols at dawn. It was a society of refined speech and graceful conversation, with the not-surprising result that Southern leaders tended to be skillful in law and politics. The Southerner too had none of the Northerner's distaste for vicarious labor; in fact it was this which made his system possible. At the top of Southern society was a landed gentry patterned on the English feudal model, with all that gentry's deep-seated mistrust of "trade." At the bottom were the slaves and between them a class of poor whites—landless, often indentured, ill-educated, and easily manipulated by the slavocracy above them.

To these innate cultural differences were added differences of geography and climate. Imagine a rectangle 1,500 miles long and barely 350 miles wide. Put mountains on one side and a hostile ocean on the other; at either end, put untracked wilderness. Draw a line across the middle of this rectangle, call it the Mason-Dixon line, and you have an accurate picture of the United States up to about 1800. Only on the narrow "border" across the middle did the two cultures meet, and even then only intermittently. Difficulties of terrain made east-west communication easier than that from north to south. As a consequence, North and South became increasingly internalized, more interested in its own regional development and in westward expansion than in communication with its neighbor north or south of the border.

The climate at the top of the rectangle was sub-arctic

*RIGHT: How to wring the last drop of sentiment from a staged bestseller: playbill for the Howard family's version of* Uncle Tom's Cabin. *The alternative title switches attention from the original hero to the main box-office attraction: Little Cordelia Howard, "the world renowned child actress". The final "grand allegorical tableau" completely ignores Tom's sufferings, to depict "Eva in Heaven".*

# PINE STREET THEATRE.

VARREY & ARNOLD, . . . . . . . . . . . . . . . . . . . . . . . . . . . . . . . MANAGERS.

PRICES OF ADMISSION—BOXES, 37½ CENTS. | PARQUETTE, 25 CENTS.
Reserved Seats in Boxes, 50 Cents.     Box Office open from 10, a. m. till 2, p. m.

## ENGAGEMENT OF THE WORLD RENOWNED CHILD ACTRESS
## LITTLE CORDELIA

# HOWARD,

AND HER TALENTED PARENTS;

## MR. & MRS. G. C. HOWARD.

They will appear in their original character of

## EVA, TOPSY AND ST. CLAIR,

As performed by them (and them only,) in the principal Cities of AMERICA, ENGLAND, IRELAND and SCOTLAND, over **ONE THOUSAND TIMES.**
The Critics of London, Edinburgh and Dublin, were unanimous in their praise of

### THE GIFTED AMERICAN CHILD.

### ALTERATION OF TIME:

The Doors will open this evening, at a quarter before 7 o'clock.     The curtain will rise at 7½.

### Monday Evening, October 10th, 1859,

Will be presented the entire original Moral Drama, dramatized expressly for the Howard's, in 6 Acts, and 30 Scenes, entitled

# UNCLE TOM'S CABIN,
## Or, THE DEATH OF EVA.

EVA, . . . . . . . . . . . . . . . . . . . . . . . . . . . . . . . . . . . . . . . . . . . . . . . . LITTLE CORDELIA HOWARD
Topsy, . . . . . . . . . Mrs. G. C. HOWARD    St. Clair, . . . . . . . . . Mr. G. C. HOWARD
In which characters they will sing their original Songs of "EVA TO HER PAPA," "I'S SO WICKED," and "ST. CLAIR TO EVA IN HEAVEN," written and composed by G. C. Howard, Esq. expressly for his family.

### As Played by them over 1000 Nights.

| | |
|---|---|
| UNCLE TOM, . . . . . . . . . . . . . . . . . . . . . . . . . . . . . . . . . . . . . . . Mr. W. PETRIE, | |
| Marks, a Lawyer, . . . . . . . Mr. Harry Linden | Gumption Cute, (a Yankee.) . . Mr. E. Varrey |
| George Harris, . . . . . . . . Mr. R. Johnston | Mr. Shelby, . . . . . . . . Mr. H. C. Raymond |
| Lagree, . . . . . . . . . . . Mr. C. E. Mathews | George Shelby, . . . . . . . . Mr. W. Marden |
| Haley, . . . . . . . . . . . . . . . Mr. Green | Deacon Perry, . . . . . . . . . Mr. W. Lomas |
| Phineas Fletcher, . . . . . . . Mr. E. Varrey | Tom Loker, . . . . . . . . . . . Mr. Curtis |
| Sambo, . . . . . . . . . . . Mr. W. S. Andrews | Alf Mann, . . . . . . . . . Mr. T. H. Shannon |
| Eliza Harris, . . . . . . . . Mrs. W. Marden | Cassey, . . . . . . . . Miss Mary A. Mitchell |
| Mrs. St. Clair, . . . . . . . . Mrs. Warden | Emeline, . . . . . . . . . . . . Miss Gillet |
| Aunt Chloe, . . . . . . . . . . . . . . . . . . | Miss Roylance |

### TABLEAUX.

The Rescue of Eva—Escape of Eliza—The Trappers Entrapped—Freeman's Defence—Eva and Tom in the Garden—Death of Eva—Last of St. Clair—Topsey Butting the Yankee—Cassey helping the Slave—The End of Uncle Tom, and the

### GRAND ALLEGORICAL TABLEAU OF
# EVA IN HEAVEN.

A spirit of celestial light in the abode of bliss eternal.

The Olneyville Omnibus will leave the Theatre every evening at the close of the performance.

*Whistling, Shouting, and Standing on the seats, most positively prohibited.*

## $100 REWARD!

### RANAWAY

From the undersigned, living on Current River, about twelve miles above Doniphan, in Ripley County, Mo., on 2nd of March, 1860, A NE GRO MAN, about 30 years old, weighs about 160 pounds; high forehead, with a scar on it; had on brown pants and coat very much worn, and an old black wool hat; shoes size No. 11.

The above reward will be given to any person who may apprehend this said negro out of the State; and fifty dollars if apprehended in this State outside of Ripley county, or $25 if taken in Ripley county.

APOS TUCKER.

(Mrs Keeley as Topsy, "I's dreful wicked.")

IN

## "SLAVE LIFE", OR "UNCLE TOM'S CABIN."

ABOVE: Reward placard for a runaway slave, from Ripley County, Missouri . . . The reward scale runs from "$25 if taken in Ripley County", to $50 if taken outside Ripley County but within Missouri, to $100 if taken outside the Missouri State line. By the mid-1850s the refusal of the Northern states to vote for a really effective "fugitive slave law", returning all escaped slaves to slave soil, was one of the South's most burning grievances.

LEFT: From abolitionist best-seller to hit musical. This publicity print for one of the innumerable musical versions of Uncle Tom's Cabin shows actress Mrs Keeley "blacked up" in the role of Topsy, ready for her tear-jerking rendering of "I's Dreful Wicked".

14

RIGHT: *Nerve center of Southern wealth: the New Orleans Cotton Exchange, by Degas. After a discouraging slump in the 1840s, the cotton market rebounded over the 1850s with prices soaring from five cents to 12 cents a pound. The net result was the breeding of a fatal over-confidence in the industrial world's dependence on Southern cotton.*

FAR RIGHT: *A visual hymn to "King Cotton", summing up the fatal delusion of the South. "What would happen if no cotton was furnished for three years?" declaimed Senator Hammond of South Carolina in 1858. "Old England would topple headlong and carry the whole civilized world with her. No, sir, you dare not make war on cotton. No power on earth dares make war upon it. Cotton is King!"*

**16**

*FAR RIGHT: The arrest of rebel slave leader Nat Turner in Southampton County, Virginia, October 1831. Turner's followers never numbered more than 60, and his rapid defeat was brought about by slaves who loyally fought for their masters.*

*BELOW: The ultimate, human source of Southern prosperity: plantation slave workers in the fields. There were 3,838,750 of them in 1860 — out of the South's total population of 11,133,361.*

and at the bottom sub-tropical, with all that implied for the vast tracts of land that lay between. Climate determined what crops could be grown, where they could be grown, what methods of farming were economical and which were not. It determined whether an economy should grow food crops for consumption or cash crops for export; ultimately, it determined whether a society stayed agricultural or turned to manufacturing and industry. By the end of the 18th century, these factors had pushed the South well on the way to becoming an essentially agrarian society, and the North an industrial one. Even so, these differences were not in themselves strong enough to have dissolved the Union—nor would they ever have done so—if other factors had not intervened.

In 1793, the cotton gin was invented—a device for removing the seeds from cotton fiber—which made possible the large-scale, profitable production of cotton.

The arrival of the cotton gin coincided with the accelerating pace of the industrial revolution and its insatiable demand for raw cotton. The factories of England and, later, New England demanded all the cotton the South could grow. The boom was on. The Cotton Belt, and hence the Slave Belt, pushed rapidly westward to the Mississippi and beyond, and as far northward as soil and climate would permit. The south rapidly became a one-crop economy based on slave labor. For the next sixty years "King Cotton" reigned supreme. The basis of Southern wealth was cotton—and the basis of profitable cotton growing was slave labor.

### Slave against Free States

When the Union was formed in 1787, some states were Slave and some were Free, but this had come about mainly by a process of natural selection. Slavery had been tried in the North, found unprofitable, and

*FAR RIGHT: General Winfield Scott's American army lands at Vera Cruz in March 1847, before marching inland to the conquest of Mexico City. The Mexican War of 1846–48 was the first outright war of conquest waged by the United States, with Mexico being deliberately baited into war by President Polk. The most valuable American gain of the war was Mexico's Pacific province of California — but the spoils of war with Mexico were immediately disputed between the free-state and slave-state factions within the American Union.*

*BELOW: This was how white Americans preferred to think of slavery, or "the peculiar institution", as it was known in the South: contented darkies in "The Old Kentucky Home" by Eastman Johnson. Perhaps this picture's most disquieting aspect is that it was painted nearly 20 years after the conflict.*

withered away. It was assumed that much the same thing would happen in the South. The Founding Fathers left slavery as a matter for each state to decide for itself, rather than as a matter to establish by Constitutional principle. No particular antagonism over the issue of slavery was anticipated, and if it should arise, then there were roughly an equal number of Free and Slave states among the original thirteen—a balance of power which would enable each section to look after its own interests.

This balance of power was maintained over the next fifteen years as equal numbers of Slave and Free states were admitted to the Union. But then came the Louisiana Purchase of 1803. It was obvious that this vast new area would rapidly fill with settlers from the more populous North. When these new territories came to clamor for admission to the Union, therefore, they would seek to enter as Free states. The balance of power would shift away from the South, severely limiting the ability of its politicians to manipulate, lobby, and filibuster.

Compromises in 1820, 1833, and 1850 managed to maintain a delicate balance of power in the Senate and, to an extent, to defuse growing sectional antagonisms. The massive population imbalance in favor of the North, however, could not be forestalled forever.

The Missouri Compromise of 1820 had left a festering anger in the South. By the terms of the Compromise, Missouri was admitted as a Slave state, but the expansion of slavery into the territories was forbidden north of 36°30′—the southern boundary of Kentucky and Virginia. This compromise line was taken as a

**20**

RIGHT: *General Winfield Scott enters Mexico City in triumph, September 1847. His direction of the war against Mexico established him as the Union's leading military commander, and he was still general-in-chief (under the President as Commander-in-Chief) as the Union's supreme crisis approached in 1860–61.*

FAR RIGHT: *General Scott in 1861. Old, infirm, and frequently bed-ridden, he had nevertheless retained all his mental faculties and proposed the "Anaconda Plan" — a combined effort of strangling blockade and converging attacks — for the defeat of the Confederacy.*

The great Texan legend: last stand of the Alamo garrison, San Antonio, March 1836. The Alamo siege won time for the Texan leader Sam Houston to muster his forces and avenge the Alamo with a crushing victory over the Mexicans at San Jacinto. The successful fight for independence by the American settlers in Texas — predominantly Southern in birth and sympathies — carved out a huge new Slave state west of the Mississippi.

standing affront by the South. There seemed to be no limit imposed on the future expansion of the Free states, whereas the westward expansion of the Slave states was blocked by the Mexican provinces of Texas, New Mexico, and California. From this time onward, the South felt increasingly on the defensive and resolved to fight all future attempts to restrict slavery.

By the 1850s, sectional rivalries had intensified yet again. The publication of *Uncle Tom's Cabin*, the rapid formation of Abolitionist and Free-state societies, the publication of abolitionist newspapers like *The Liberator*, Nat Turner's abortive slave uprising—everywhere the South looked it saw itself hemmed in and threatened. More than that, in every economic and

demographic category, the North was outstripping the South. Dixie had become a static agrarian economy unalterably opposed to high tariffs, subsidies for shipping, and national currency and banking. The North, as an expanding industrial economy, was struggling to attain exactly the goals the Southerners despised.

Relations were further strained by the Kansas-Nebraska Act of 1854, which in effect repealed the Missouri Compromise and made possible the further expansion of slavery. The Act was a triumph for Southern political skills, but one which enraged idealists in the North and convinced them of Southern intractability. In the same year, the Republican party

was born. This gave a convenient focus to the anti-slavery sentiments of the North. In the years that followed, the outrages of "Bleeding Kansas" and the lonely acts of fanatics like John Brown, who tried to start a slave uprising in the South, convinced moderate Southerners that their only hope of preserving their society lay, not in arbitration, but in secession.

The two societies had in any case different views about the Union. The colonies had joined together in the first place out of mutual interest. To the North, that Union was inviolate, a federation of member states under a strong central government; to the South, the Union had always seemed a looser bond, a confederation of sovereign states. If the Union no longer served

*FAR LEFT: California bound — prospectors haul their wagons and pack-mules over a hair-raising Rocky Mountain pass during the 1849 Gold Rush, a mass migration which ruined any chance of a gradual, peaceful settlement of the West and its political future.*

*LEFT: After the Kansas-Nebraska Act of 1854 became law, leaving the future statehood of Kansas to be decided by "popular sovereignty", "Bleeding Kansas" became a battleground between free-state and slave-state extremists. Repeated atrocities and acts of retaliation were committed by both factions. In this depiction, free-state settlers are gunned down in the "Marais des Cygnes Massacre" of May 19, 1858.*

*LEFT: By the middle 1850s, the expanding American railroad network had already pushed its first tentacles west of the Mississippi. It was to transform the prosperity of the states through which it would run — earning the scheme the implacable hostility of the South, excluded by geography.*

*BELOW: Gold fever: panning for gold on a Californian river, 1848. The discovery of gold in the Sacramento Valley during the peace negotiations with Mexico was a disaster for those who hoped that a free state/slave state compromise could be achieved, given time. By unleashing a flood of gold-hungry adventurers from the Mississippi to the Pacific, the California Gold Rush of 1849 highlighted the need for an early settlement of the problem of slavery in the shrinking western "frontier".*

mutual interests, then any member state or states had the right to dissolve the bonds of that Union.

In 1858 and 1859, the South lost the balance of power in the Senate and with this, its ability to block legislation inimical to its interests. The final straw was the election in 1860 of a Republican President—Abraham Lincoln. Lincoln's views on slavery were moderate—even conciliatory—but the South saw his election as a clear signal that the time had come for the parting of ways.

From Lincoln's election in November 1859 to his inauguration in March 1860, seven states seceded from the Union. Another four waited nervously in the wings, watching the Government's reaction to the formation of the Confederate States Government, complete with a working Cabinet and a rival President—Jefferson Davis of Mississippi. Never has an American President taken office amid such a supreme crisis. With the Confederacy already in existence, Lincoln's hopes of preserving the Union by negotiation lay in ruins. Now he could only try to prevent more Slave states from joining the Confederacy without, at the same time, provoking outright war. The most sensitive point was at Charleston, South Carolina, the heart of secessionist territory. Here a tiny Union garrison on the island of Fort Sumter lay trapped in a ring of Confederate guns.

PRIMARY CAUSES of the REBELLION.
CANE, COTTON AND the NEGRO.

FAR LEFT: *The making of an abolitionist legend. John Brown as the camera saw him: a hard-faced fanatic, ruthless leader of murder squads and lynchings in the night . . .* EXTREME FAR LEFT: *Passing into myth, John Brown depicted as a whitebearded saintly martyr blessing a slave woman and her child on his way to the scaffold in 1859, after his ill-fated raid on Harper's Ferry. The use here of the slogan* Sic Semper Tyrannis *("So May It Ever Be With Tyrants") as abolitionist propaganda is a bitter irony. The same words would be shouted by John Wilkes Booth after he assassinated Lincoln, "The Great Liberator", in April 1865.*

LEFT: *Wash drawing by J.E. Taylor: an allegory on the theme of black slave, white cotton. "Cane, Cotton and the Negro" was the original sour caption to this picture, "Primary Cause of the Rebellion". But it was not true. The Civil War at its outset was not a crusade against slavery, but against the claimed right of the rebel Southern states to secede from the American Union.*

RIGHT: "Honest Abe and Victory!" The Republic band-wagon begins to roll in September 1860, two months before the election which sent Lincoln to the White House. The excitement of the campaign was generated by the supreme opportunity offered the Republicans by the yawning gulf in the Democractic Party. Hannibal Hamlin, Lincoln's running-mate as Vice-President, was a sound Republican moderate and an Easterner, while Lincoln stood for the ebullient energy of the Northwest.

FAR RIGHT: A beardless Abraham Lincoln, at the time he fought the fateful 1860 Presidential election. He claimed that he grew his famous beard on the advice of a little girl — "to give me more dignity". Lincoln's awkward manners and gangling appearance — his 6ft 4 inches were accentuated by a tall "stovepipe" hat — dismayed even staunch Republicans, and many months passed before Lincoln's true stature as a national leader began to emerge.

# RALLY! RALLY!!
## OUR FLAG IS THERE!

The Republicans of old Franklin will erect a Liberty-Pole in Bloomingrove,

## SATURDAY, SEPT. 8th, 1860,

From which will be flung to the breeze, a NATIONAL FLAG, emblazoned with the names of the working-men's friends,

## LINCOLN AND HAMLIN!

"Forever float that standard sheet!
Where is the foe but falls before us,
With Freedom's soil beneath our feet,
And Freedom's banner streaming o'er us!"

## SPEAKING

By Hon. NELSON TRUSLER, Elector for the 5th Congressional District; JEREMIAH M. WILSON, Esq., Candidate for Common Pleas Judge; JOHN C. WHITRIDGE, Esq., Candidate for Common Pleas Prosecutor, and others. A Grand Procession by the

## WIDE AWAKES
## AND
## LINCOLN RANGERS!

Music by the Brookville Military Band, the best Band in the State.
Come with music and banners; come in wagons, on horse back and a foot; come and bring your wives, your sons and your daughters with you, and let us make the welkin ring with shouts for

## Honest Abe and Victory!

Pole raising at 12 oclock, M. Speaking to commence at 1 o'clock P. M.
Blooming Grove, Ind., August 28, 1860.

# 2  The New Nation: 1861

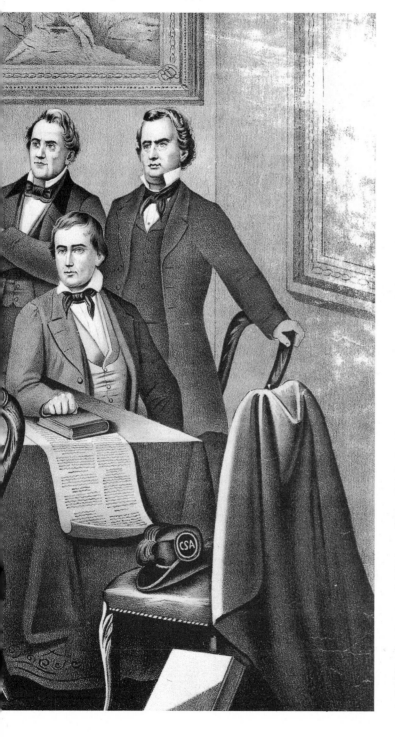

IN CREATING THE GOVERNMENT of their new Confederacy, the delegates at Montgomery, Alabama, had more need for haste than the moral victory to be won by anticipating Lincoln's inauguration. Until every one of the wavering Slave states yet to secede had been peacefully seduced from the Union, it was vital to prevent hot-headed South Carolina from going to war on her own. If South Carolina pressed her claim to the Union-held Forts Moultrie and Sumter in Charleston Harbor, or tried to take the forts by force, war with the mutilated Union would be inevitable. And even before the Montgomery convention met in February 1861, the expiring administration of Pres-

ident Buchanan had given disturbing signs that the Union was prepared to fight for the Charleston forts.

**The Charleston Forts**
The forts came into prominence the day after Lincoln's victory was announced. On November 7, Colonel John L. Gardner, commanding the Charleston forts, had prudently ordered ammunition and weapons to be shipped from the Federal arsenal to Fort Moultrie, but an angry mob swamped the Charleston waterfront and thwarted the move. When this was followed by a stiff protest to Washington, Gardner was hastily removed and was replaced by Major Robert Anderson: a

*LEFT: Like Lincoln, Kentucky-born: Jefferson Davis, President of the Confederate States. His wife recalled that when he told her that he was to be Confederate President, he spoke "as a man might speak of a sentence of death". Yet, though he had not sought this supreme office, he would not shirk it. As he traveled to Montgomery for his inauguration, Davis pledged that "I am ready, as I always have been, to redeem by pledges to you and the South by shedding every drop of blood in your cause".*

*FAR LEFT: Davis and the Confederate States Cabinet. left to right: Navy Secretary Stephen P. Mallory (Florida); Attorney General Judah P. Benjamin (Louisiana); Secretary of War Leroy P. Walker (Alabama); President Davis (Mississippi); General Robert E. Lee (Virginia); Postmaster General John F. Reagan (Texas); Treasury Secretary Christopher Memminger (South Carolina); Vice-President Stephens (Georgia); Secretary of State Robert Toombs (Georgia). When David formed the first Confederate Cabinet in February 1861, Virginia was still in the Union and Robert E. Lee, a colonel, was on his way back to Washington from Texas — hoping against hope that his home state would not secede.*

Southerner, Kentucky-born, and married to a Georgian wife. Anderson's initial brief was to report on the state of the forts and the mood of the citizens of Charleston, and to avoid conflict at all costs. Grudgingly accepting the olive branch which Anderson's appointment so obviously represented, the South Carolina delegates in Washington gave Buchanan a written assurance on December 9 that no move would be made against the forts—"provided that no reinforcements shall be sent into those forts & their relative military status remains as at present."

Anderson's summation of the situation, meanwhile, was that Fort Moultrie, on the mainland, was indefensible; and that island Fort Sumter, though unfinished, offered the only real chance of maintaining a Union presence at Charleston. Fort Sumter, however, was unmanned. At any moment, boatloads of South Carolinans could row across and take possession, but if Anderson were to anticipate the danger and occupied Sumter himself, the move would inevitably be regarded as hostile. The hapless Anderson got no help from Washington; they ordered him not to abandon the forts, not to occupy Fort Sumter, not to take any provocative action, yet to defend himself if attacked. It was the mounting excitement in Charleston, culminating in South Carolina's secession on December 20, which decided Anderson. Believing that there was no other way of doing what the government wanted him to do, Anderson occupied Fort Sumter with his entire force—

eighty-five officers and men—on December 26.

By occupying Sumter, Anderson had at least prevented a clash between his men and the secessionists on the mainland. To the inevitable protest from Charleston, President Buchanan could reply that the agreement of December 9 not to violate the *status quo* had been nullified by South Carolina's secession. Southern hopes that Buchanan would submit to moral blackmail, and order Anderson to abandon Fort Sumter in hopes of preventing more states from seceding, were dashed. On the vigorous advice of Lieutenant-General Winfield Scott, Commander-in-Chief of the Union Army, Buchanan's mood hardened. Deciding not to deprive his successor of the Union's last garrison in rebel South Carolina, Buchanan ordered that the Fort Sumter garrison was not only to be supplied by sea, but reinforced.

The attempt was made on January 9, using a chartered steamer, *Star of the West*, and it was a fiasco. The last-minute message from the US War Department, informing Anderson of what was afoot and authorizing him to open fire if *Star of the West* should be molested, never reached Fort Sumter. When *Star of the West* headed in towards Fort Sumter, she came under crossfire from secessionist guns at Fort Moultrie and Morris Island. Anderson, fearful of starting a war, did not open fire on the rebel batteries. Bereft of support from Fort Sumter, the skipper of *Star of the West* put about and headed back out to sea.

*Lonely Fort Jefferson on the Dry Tortugas, midway between the tip of Florida and Cuba — one of the forts which, thanks to the US Navy, the Union had no trouble in holding.*

The "bomb-proof caverns", or casemates, of Fort Sumter — in which Anderson's garrison sheltered from the Confederate fire. Apart from the desperate shortage of supplies, which would have obliged him to surrender within days even if the Confederates had not fired a single shot, Anderson's problems were twofold. Fort Sumter was never meant to endure sustained converging fire from the mainland, and he lacked the manpower to crew all the guns in the fort.

February 1861: Confederate gunners man a battery of heavy "Columbiad" guns, abandoned by the Union withdrawal from its southernmost coastal forts, covering the entrance to Pensacola Bay, Florida. This formidable-looking array of heavy ordnance is, however, wholly unprotected from plunging shellfire — quite unlike the Union batteries, encased in masonry casemates in island Fort Sumter at Charleston.

36

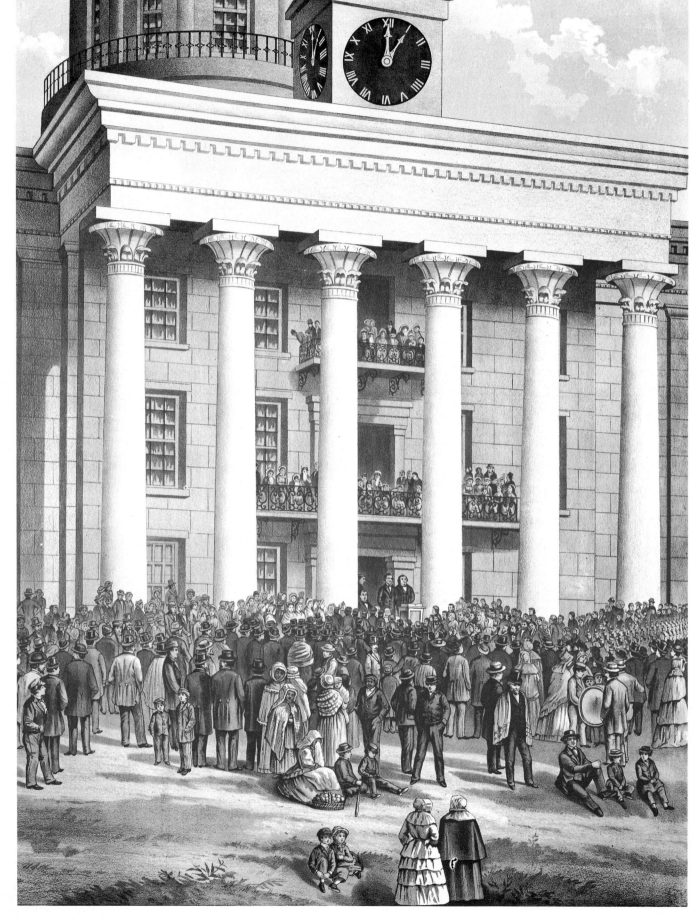

RIGHT: Montgomery, Alabama: Jefferson Davis takes the Oath of Office as President of the Confederate States, February 18, 1861. Most who watched were deeply moved by the sincerity of the occasion. One of them was the correspondent for the New York Herald: "God does not permit evil to be done with such earnest solemnity, such all-pervading trust in His Providence, as was exhibited by the whole people on that day".

FAR RIGHT: Major Robert Anderson, commanding the Union garrison at Fort Sumter. Anderson had been artillery instructor at West Point.

In a sense, the first shot fired at *Star of the West*—a Union ship flying the Union flag—was the first shot of the Civil War. One of the shells had actually hit *Star of the West*, happily without inflicting casualties. Had any loss of life resulted from the secessionist fire, open hostilities might well have resulted; but an uneasy truce was maintained at Charleston after rapid negotiations between Anderson and Governor Francis W. Pickens. The truth was that in this second week of January, South Carolina was still more or less on her own. Anderson was not prepared to start a war, and Pickens knew that South Carolina lacked the means to do so alone, eager though he was to take Fort Sumter and complete South Carolina's seizure of independence.

## Davis in Confederate Control

Within four weeks the scene had completely changed. South Carolina was now a member state of the Confederacy, whose new constitution prevented any individual member state from waging war. Moreover, President Davis was determined that he, as Head of the Confederate Government, would decide what should be done at Charleston—not Governor Pickens. To this end, Davis sent one of his newly-appointed generals down to Charleston to take command in the name of the Confederate Government. He chose Brigadier Pierre G. T. Beauregard, a Louisianan whose last command in the Union Army had been Superintendent of West Point, with the rank of captain. Beauregard reached Charleston on March 3, and immediately began the tactful work of re-siting the South Carolinan guns so that their fire—if and when it came—would be directed to maximum advantage.

The dispatch of Beauregard to Charleston revealed some of the formidable talents which Jefferson Davis took with him to the Confederate Presidency. He could judge and act with firmness and determination, and his first success as President was to shift the control of events at Charleston into his own hands. The choice of Beauregard also showed Davis at his best in giving the right job to the right man. As a politician, Davis knew that he needed a diplomat-soldier at Charleston whose arrival would not offend the touchy South Carolinans. Beauregard, with his polished Creole manners, was the best possible representative of the new Confederate Army that Davis could have picked.

Davis enjoyed another priceless advantage, which Abraham Lincoln did not have. Davis was a former professional soldier himself, who had served with distinction and still held the rank of Major-General; the Confederacy was headed by an astute politician who thought like a soldier. Davis knew that the problem of Fort Sumter was without precedent in modern military history; but he also knew that any problem connected with siege warfare was best placed before an engineer rather than an artilleryman. Beauregard had served as an engineer officer on General Scott's staff during the Mexican War. Lacking such specialist knowledge, Lincoln would have to learn from painful experience about the workings of the military mind.

All these talents were needed, for Davis became President at the moment when the first run of seceding states had petered out. These were the cotton states,

whose hatred of Northern duplicity and greed had always been strongest, and their secession had been prompted by a provocation no greater than the election of a Republican President. But now there was a lull, as the remaining Slave states—Arkansas, Tennessee, North Carolina, Missouri, Kentucky, Maryland, Delaware, and above all the "Old Dominion", Virginia—waited to see how Lincoln would proceed against the Confederacy in general, and Fort Sumter in particular.

To gather these states safely into the Confederacy, Davis was determined to maintain a front of mixed resolution and responsibility, with the hottest heads kept tactfully but firmly under control. His initial treatment of South Carolina reflected this determination, and so did his appointments to Cabinet posts. He chose a team which could not be condemned as "fire-eating" secessionists (with the sole exception of Robert Toombs of Georgia, Secretary of State), or as a clique of personal cronies from the cotton-planter aristocracy. Three of the six members of his Cabinet had been born

abroad; two were complete strangers to Davis, whom he chose on local advice; and all of them were known to have voiced their reluctance to break with the old Union. Davis himself had neither sought the Presidency nor shirked it when he was chosen for the job. That was the image he wanted his cabinet team to project and that, by and large, was what he got. It was not only a steady team but a *subordinate* team. From the beginning to the end of the Confederacy's existence, Davis never had the same problems of keeping his Cabinet in order that bedeviled Abraham Lincoln in Washington.

## Brotherhood in War

In his inaugural speech on March 4, 1861, Lincoln stated the vital principle on which his administration was to stand. This was the disconcerting argument that the Confederacy did not exist. There *were* no Confederate states, because no state had the right to secede, and those Americans who considered secession possible—let alone workable—were deluded. The so-called

*Confederate troops cheerfully occupy an abandoned Union fort in Texas, March 1861. Lincoln's government wisely decided to accept the inevitable and declined to contest the secession of Texas, concentrating on the more accessible flashpoint of Fort Sumter on the Atlantic coast.*

*A specimen delusion of what the war would be like: "Off For The War". The Civil War was notable for determinedly romantic artistic tastes — all the more desperately pursued after the first slaughter-battles of 1862.*

RIGHT: *Confederates trapping the crew of a boat of the Potomac Fleet.*

BELOW: *Brigadier General J.S. Wadsworth and his staff. Wadsworth distinguished himself as a Union general and served so efficiently at the Battle of Bull Run that he was made a brigadier general. His division held off Confederate forces for three days at Gettysburg, despite great losses; Wadsworth was killed at Chancellorsville.*

FAR RIGHT, TOP: *Reading the war news on Broadway. New Yorkers search in vain for news of the early, crushing Union victory which had been so confidently expected as the armies began to march.*

FAR RIGHT, BOTTOM: *The destruction of the Federal merchantman* Harvey Birch *by the Confederate war sloop* Nashville.

Confederate states were not mortal foes of the Union: they were still part of the Union. The American states currently denying allegiance to the Union did not represent "foreign" or "enemy" soil: it was Union soil, now and forever, and by his Presidential oath Lincoln was sworn to keep it so.

Many loyal Americans found this viewpoint startling. Armed enemies were armed enemies, and the soil held by enemies was enemy soil; how could the *fact* of secession and the formation of the Confederacy be denied? The Union generals, in particular, were to find Lincoln's vision of "no enemy soil" particularly hard to grasp; indeed, most of them never did. Over two years later, when the victor of Gettysburg exhorted his troops to "drive the invader from our soil," Lincoln raged, "Will our generals never get that idea out of their heads? The whole country is our soil!" But by stressing this concept in his inaugural address, Lincoln knew precisely what he was doing. For the immediate present, he was repeating his assurance that the still unseceded states had nothing to fear from his administration; for the future, he was assuring the malcontents of the South that their return to the Union fold would not be punished with reprisals.

When it came to the present point of confrontation—Fort Sumter—Lincoln put his message indirectly but unmistakably. "The power entrusted to me will be used to hold, occupy, and possess the property, and places belonging to the Government, and to collect the duties and imposts." In other words, the Union would hold what it had, including Fort Sumter. Lincoln apparently had not yet realized that Anderson was still at Fort Sumter only by courtesy of the truce with the city of Charleston. Having stated his policies to both North and South, Lincoln then pledged that if war should come it would not be started by the Union. But before the day was out Lincoln was informed that Fort Sumter could only be supplied by a military operation, and that supplies were needed within weeks rather than months.

By mid-April at the latest, when Anderson's last supplies had been consumed, he would have no option but to surrender. Without the dispatch of seaborne supplies, Fort Sumter would inevitably fall to the Confederates. Any ships carrying supplies to Sumter would, of course, be in mortal danger from the encircling Confederate batteries, unless those batteries were suppressed by naval gunfire; or unless Union troops were landed to take the batteries and spike the guns. Whichever way the problem of supplying Fort Sumter was sliced, it came down to preparing for an act of war. And such an act was bound to swing the balance in Virginia's secession convention, which was still in session and watching for the first hostile move by the North. Where the "Old Dominion" went, the other hesitating Slave states were likely to follow.

## Lincoln's Early Problems

During his exhausting first weeks as President, Lincoln got little help from his Cabinet, nearly all of whose members were in favor of abandoning Fort Sumter and facing conflict with the Confederacy on more favorable ground. Lincoln's biggest problem was his late rival for

the Presidential nomination—Seward, now Secretary of State. Seward's behavior in March 1861 was extraordinary—negotiating directly with the three Confederate emissaries sent to Washington, holding secret interviews, making unauthorized promises in the President's name, and generally behaving as though Seward was the then real maker of government policy and not Lincoln. It took until April 1 before Lincoln asserted himself, bluntly informing Seward that Cabinet policy would be executed by the President, not by Seward. And Lincoln showed that he meant what he said by bringing a rapid end to all the damaging speculation over what was going to happen at Fort Sumter.

Lincoln's aim was to demonstrate to all Americans, as to the world, that the Confederacy, and not the Union, was prepared to start a shooting war. He now chose to send formal notice to the Confederate Government that supplies would be sent to the Fort Sumter garrison, supported by Union troops and warships. This was to be no furtive blockade-running, such as had been tried with *Star of the West* back in January, but a deliberate operation conducted out in the open, with the Con-

federates fully briefed in advance and left to take what action they dared.

## Count-down to War

On April 8, US War Department clerk Robert S. Chew reached Charleston with a copy of Lincoln's orders to Captain Gustavus V. Fox, commanding the expedition. These were concise. If Fox found the Union flag still flying over Sumter, and if the fort had not been attacked, he was to seek an interview with Governor Pickens and read him the following message:

*I am directed by the President of the United States to notify you to expect an attempt will be made to supply Fort Sumter with provisions only; and that, if such attempt be not resisted, no effort to throw in men, arms or ammunition will be made without further notice, or in case of an attack upon the Fort.*

This message was no declaration of war—merely a statement that the Union was determined to maintain, indefinitely if need be, its garrison at Fort Sumter. The moral burden for starting the war was thus effectively

*The shape of things to come. In captured Richmond, Union officers pose proudly on the steps of Jefferson Davis' former home. It had taken them three years and 11 months to get there.*

*These uniforms represent the hopes of those who organized the armies of both sides. Clothing was thought to have an important bearing on the soldiers' morale, but in reality, regulation dress was never fully observed. The Confederate soldiers, in particular, were poor and raggedness was normal, and both armies suffered terribly from chronic shortages of overcoats and boots.*

44

The 1861 "Fourth of July" Parade in Washington, less than three weeks before the shattering humiliation of 1st Bull Run. Men of the "Garibaldi Guard", their uniforms aping those of Italian 'Bersaglieri', pass in review before President Lincoln (standing by the flagpole). The seated officer is the aging, infirm, yet resolute Union General-in-Chief, Winfield Scott.

Du Pont's Upper Brandywine Powder Mills, Delaware, in 1854. Northern factories were grim counterparts to the South's plantations, and the sinews of Northern victory in the coming conflict. By 1860 the North had some 110,843 factories of all sizes, against only 20,631 in the South. In the same year, the all-important index of capital investment in industrial production came to a staggering $866.75 million in the North; the South's figure was a beggarly $95.8 million.

shifted from Lincoln to Jefferson Davis. When consulted by Davis, the Confederate Cabinet agreed that if the Sumter garrison should be replenished or reinforced, or even if it were merely withdrawn without having surrendered first, the result would be a humiliation to Confederate pride. The Cabinet advised Davis that he should order the capture of Fort Sumter before the Union expeditionary force arrived. There was only one dissenting voice, which interestingly enough, came from the former fire-eater, Robert Toombs. "Mr President," he told Davis, "at this time it is suicide, murder, and will lose us every friend at the North. You will wantonly strike a hornet's nest which extends from mountains to ocean, and legions now quiet will swarm out and sting us to death. It is unnecessary; it puts us in the wrong; it is fatal."

Lincoln himself could not have put it better, and Davis was shaken enough to put a modifying phrase into the orders he sent General Beauregard on April 10. *If Beauregard had no doubt* that Lincoln's emissary was genuine, he was to demand Anderson's surrender, and proceed to attack only if Anderson refused to haul down his flag. Beauregard's written surrender demand, and Anderson's written refusal were, accordingly, exchanged on April 11. There was a flurry of last-minute negotiations to explore the possibility of Anderson evacuating the fort on April 15, by which date his provisions would have run out; but the approach of the Union flotilla was detected. Anderson's cautious agreement to evacuate Sumter on the 15th, provided that he had received neither provisions nor new orders from his Government in the meantime, was now interpreted by Beauregard's emissaries as an obvious play for time. In a lamplit farewell on Sumter wharf, at 3.20am on April 12, Anderson was told that a preliminary bombardment would be opened in one hour's time.

As it turned out, the Confederates were ten minutes late. The emissaries had landed at Fort Johnson, the nearest battery. There the battery commander invited visiting Congressman Roger Pryor of Virginia to fire the first shot, but he declined—"I could not fire the first gun of the war." That fateful honor therefore passed to Lieutenant Henry S. Farley. At 4.30am on Friday, April 12, 1861, the first shell burst over Fort Sumter and the American Civil War began.

*The Confederate General Pierre Gustave Toutant Beauregard. It was wholly typical of the developing conflict that Major Robert Anderson and Beauregard were old West Point acquaintances, soon to become enemies. When Beauregard was a cadet at West Point, Anderson was so impressed with Beauregard's ability he appointed him as assistant instructor.*

# 3 From Fort Sumter to First Bull Run: 1861

**A**N ELEMENT OF BITTER FARCE clings to the first battle of the American Civil War: the Confederate bombardment of Fort Sumter. It was a cruel illusion, giving no hint at all of the carnage which was to follow. The bombardment raged for roughly thirty-six hours, with about 4,000 shells being fired—but not one mortal soul on either side was killed until after Anderson's surrender in the late afternoon of April 13. Then, as the Union garrison prepared to march out of the fort shortly after noon on April 14, a spark from a saluting gun landed on a pile of powder cartridges, killing Private Daniel Hough and injuring five others, one of whom died in hospital five days later.

## The Fall of Sumter

Throughout the bombardment, Anderson was sustained by the knowledge that he was not expected to fight to the last man and the last round—merely to do enough to save the Union's honor, and expose the Confederates as the aggressors. This he could do, but little more. Fort Sumter had been built to dominate the seaward approach to Charleston, not to endure converging fire from the land. Although the garrison's position was hopeless, it was not fatal. Fort Sumter was strongly built: its brick walls were five feet thick, with the two lower tiers of guns mounted in casemates—chambers with a narrow embrasure for each gun, each protected by a massive shell of masonry. Anderson's dilemma was

FAR LEFT: Beauregard's "circle of fire" explodes on Fort Sumter. This painting shows the Confederate bombardment at its height on the second day, April 13, 1861. Muzzle flashes stab from Sumter's lower gunports, from where Anderson's men tried in vain to knock out the encircling batteries. The bombardment lasted some 36 hours; over 4,000 shells were fired without the loss of a single life on either side until Anderson agreed to surrender on the afternoon of April 13.

LEFT: Fort Sumter's fall sent a rallying call throughout the North with the moral comfort that the Southern "rebels" had been the first to start a shooting war. This is a typical Northern propaganda-dream of the day when "The Old Flag Again Waves Over Sumter".

that the only guns which could be brought to bear on the nearest Confederate batteries were all on the upper tier, mounted *en barbette*—out in the open, intended to fire over the parapet. And these were the guns most exposed to plunging fire from mortar shells.

From the moment he occupied Fort Sumter back in December, Anderson knew that he had far more guns— forty-eight in all—than he had men to serve them. He had walled up the embrasures on the middle tier and intended to fight the siege from the lower tier, which offered his men the most shelter. On two occasions, however, men stole up to fire guns from the upper tier, with spectacular results in the case of the 7½-ton 10-inch "Columbiad", whose recoil sent it into a backward somersault. But Anderson could do nothing to prevent Confederate shells from setting the wooden barracks ablaze in the central courtyard and his decision to sur-

render, on the afternoon of the 13th, was assisted by the danger of fire reaching Sumter's main magazine.

For his part, Beauregard had made excellent use of the time and the zealous manpower at his disposal; roughly 7,000 Confederates, against Anderson's force of eight-five soldiers and forty-three civilians. Beauregard had also adopted the latest tactic, introduced by the British and French in the Crimea only six years before, of giving key batteries armored protection. The Confederate battery on Morris Island had an ironclad shield, from which frustrated gunners in Fort Sumter watched their solid shot rebound harmlessly. Fort Moultrie had been given an equally effective protective shield—of massed cotton bales, as if to symbolize what the developing conflict was all about. Beauregard directed the bombardment with old-time chivalry, exacting no reprisals for the two errant shots from Fort

# VOLUNTEERS WANTED!

**1776!** **1861!**

## AN ATTACK UPON WASHINGTON ANTICIPATED!!

# THE COUNTRY TO THE RESCUE!

## A REGIMENT FOR SERVICE

# UNDER THE FLAG OF THE UNITED STATES

IS BEING FORMED  IN JEFFERSON COUNTY.

 # NOW IS THE TIME TO BE ENROLLED!

Patriotism and love of Country alike demand a ready response from every man capable of bearing arms in this trying hour, to sustain not merely the existence of the Government, but to vindicate the honor of that Flag so ruthlessly torn by traitor hands from the walls of Sumter.

## RECRUITING RENDEZVOUS

Are open in the village of WATERTOWN, and at all the principal villages in the County, for the formatiom of Companies, or parts of Companies.  ☞ Officers to be immediately elected by those enrolled.

WATERTOWN, APRIL 20, 1861.          **WM. C. BROWNE**, Col. Comd'g 35th Regiment.

Ingalls, Brockway & Beebee, Printers, Reformer Office, Watertown.

*A post-Sumter recruiting poster for the 35th Regiment. An interesting point is the linking of 1861 with 1776. In 1861, it was the Confederacy, not the Union, which claimed that secession was no more than a repeat of the American colonists' rejection of British rule in 1776. Note also the play on Northern fears that the Confederates were about to attack Washington.*

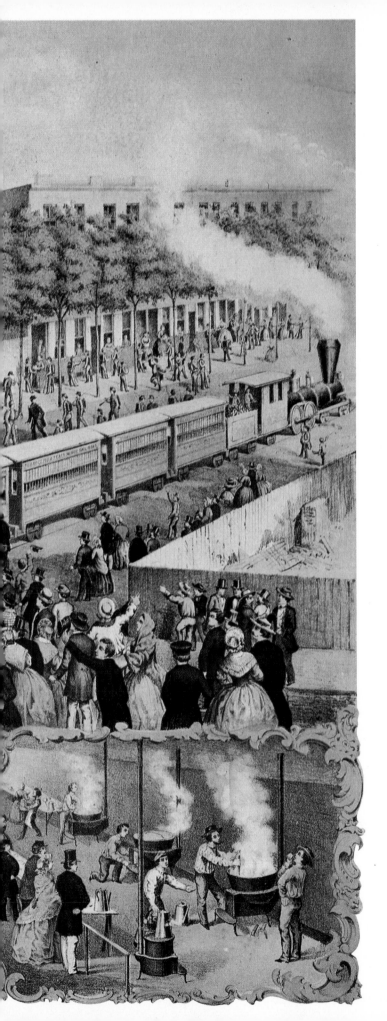

*Raw Union troops embark
for the training camps.
Lincoln's call to arms on
April 15, 1861, required
loyal states to contribute
75,000 militiamen for the
restoration of the Union. By
the end of the war the Union
would have put nearly 2
million men into the field.*

*RIGHT: War comes to Virginia in summer 1861, as the probing tips of the rival forces make contact. Here the victim is a US Cavalry dragoon, trapped and sabred by irregular Virginian rough-riders.*

Sumter which accidentally hit a building flying a hospital flag. He willingly permitted Anderson and his valiant garrison to embark for the North aboard the Union flotilla. The latter had been unable to intervene in the battle because of a high sea.

Fort Sumter's surrender had an electrifying effect in both North and South. The news that "They have fired on the Flag" did for the North what John Brown's raid on Harper's Ferry had done for the South in 1859. It released a unifying burst of patriotic anger. On April 14, Stephen Douglas called on Lincoln at the White House, heard Lincoln's proclamation asking the states of the Union for 75,000 volunteers—which was issued the following day—and urged Lincoln to make the figure 200,000 instead. The two men then went to a map and Douglas suggested various important strategic points that needed strengthening at once: Washington, Harper's Ferry, Fort Monroe at the tip of Virginia's Yorktown Peninsula, and Cairo at the southern tip of Illinois, where the Mississippi and Ohio rivers met. Douglas then issued a public statement affirming that regardless of his political opposition to Lincoln, the Northern Democrats would support Lincoln's Government in the coming struggle.

## Virginia Casts Her Lot

This was welcome news, for on April 16 Governor John Letcher of Virginia bluntly rejected Lincoln's first call to arms as an outrageous violation of the Constitution. So too did the Governors of North Carolina, Kentucky, Tennessee, Arkansas, and Missouri. Even before the Virginia convention formally voted for secession on April 17, plans for the seizure of the Federal arsenal at Harper's Ferry had been secretly laid. The Virginia militia descended on Harper's Ferry on the 18th, forcing the lone company of US troops there to evacuate the arsenal after carrying out what demolitions they could. Thus, within a week of the first shot at Fort Sumter, Virginia had not only voted to quit the Union but had seized the northern entrance to the Shenandoah Valley, the mountain corridor slanting southwestwards through the heart of the "Old Dominion." Though the convention vote for secession did not become formal until ratified by popular referendum on May 23, Virginia was effectively a member of the Confederacy as from April 17.

The secession of Virginia was a major blow to Lincoln's hopes. The most respected state of the old Union had joined the Confederacy, and thus established

the Confederacy's northern border on the Potomac River. This effectively placed the Federal capital at Washington in the front line. Virginia was also by far the most advanced industrial state south of the Mason-Dixon line, and the Tredegar Iron Works at Richmond remained the mainspring of the Confederacy's industrial production throughout the war. Apart from transforming the Confederacy's strategic prospects, Virginia's secession deprived the Union of two other priceless military assets, Colonel Robert E. Lee and Major Thomas J. Jackson. This pair was destined for

immortality as the most gifted military partnership since the Duke of Marlborough and Prince Eugene 150 years before. When their mother-state seceded Lee was in Washington, commanding the US 1st Cavalry, and Jackson was on the teaching staff of the Virginia Military Institute at Lexington.

Apart from his matchless achievements as a Confederate general, Robert E. Lee came to symbolize the whole tragedy of the American Civil War. He had been in Texas when that state seceded back in March, commanding the 2nd Cavalry, and had briefly been a

FAR LEFT: The South's greatest war asset — Robert E. Lee, the Confederate legend incarnate. By the New Year of 1863, the paramount importance of defeating Lee and the Army of Northern Virginia had repeatedly inhibited Lincoln's War Cabinet from pouring reinforcements into the West to exploit the considerable Northern successes already won there.

LEFT: Northern recruiting parade. A company of gaudily-clad "Yankee Doodle Dandies", complete with white top hats, drums up volunteers after Sumter's fall. The spring and early summer of 1861 were months of heady delusion in both North and South, alive with vague yet stirring dreams of military romance and glory. The terrible reality of modern warfare had yet to strike home.

*ABOVE: April 19, 1861 — marching through Baltimore en route for Washington, the 6th Massachusetts Regiment is forced to defend itself from stoning by a pro-Confederate mob. The riot and the ensuing shooting produced the first fatalities of the Civil War. Four soldiers and 12 rioters were killed.*

Confederate prisoner of war, flatly refusing to renounce his commission as a Union officer and join the Confederacy. To the last, Lee had hoped that his state would stay in the Union; his devotion to the Union was exceeded only by his devotion to Virginia. Back in Washington after his release by the Texans, Lee was welcomed by Army Commander-in-Chief Winfield Scott, who fully recognized Lee's talent and wanted to appoint him as the next commander of the US Army. With Lincoln's approval, Lee was offered the post on

April 18 but refused: "I cannot fight against my native state." Resigning his commission in the US Army, Lee crossed the Potomac into Virginia, hoping to live quietly at his Arlington home and fight only in Virginia's defence.

**Maryland Attempts Neutrality**

Lincoln, meanwhile, had to ensure the loyalty or at least the neutrality of the border states. Foremost among these was Maryland, which completely sur-

LEFT: *An early attempt at photo-propaganda? A greatcoated Confederate offers his water canteen to a wounded Union Zouave. The pristine condition of the uniforms suggests that the picture was taken in the opening months of the war.*

BELOW: *The ugly face of war. Union troops try to attack a column of Confederate prisoners, captured in outpost fighting, as they are paraded through the streets of Washington.*

Both sides aped the more colorful uniforms of European armies, particularly those of the Imperial French Army (made familiar by the Crimean War of 1854–56). French zouave costume was a notable favorite. Here is a detachment of the "New York Fire Zouaves", recruited from volunteer firemen. This was the regiment which gave the North its first war hero: Elmer Ellsworth, killed during the occupation of Alexandria, Virginia, on May 14, 1861.

RIGHT: *Sharp-eyed Texas Rangers (loyal to the Union despite the secession of their state) ride deeper into Virginia on reconnaissance, probing westward from Alexandria in the direction of Fairfax.*

BELOW: *The shame of the "BCD", or Bad Conduct Discharge. To the derisive beat of the "Rogue's March", stripped of buttons and rank badges, with bayonets at his back and a guard with arms reversed in shame, a defaulter is paraded through downtown Washington before being mustered out of the Union Army in disgrace. Drunkenness and misconduct in the face of the enemy were the usual crimes for which this humiliation was ordained.*

rounded Washington. Maryland had a pro-Union Governor but widespread popular support for the Confederacy. Worse, Washington's only rail link with the North ran through Baltimore; troops being shipped to the capital by rail had to march through that hostile city from one railway station to the other. On April 19, the 6th Massachusetts Regiment had to fight its way through Baltimore against a pro-Confederate mob, leaving four soldiers and twelve rioters killed and many more wounded—the first real casualties of the war. With Lincoln determined, if necessary, to put the whole of Maryland under martial law in order to get the troops through, it was largely due to Governor Thomas B. Hicks that the Maryland legislature decided against secession. Hicks put it bluntly: either stay in the Union

under a front of neutrality, taking no active part in the war with the South; or face an indefinite, humiliating future under military rule.

Lincoln then turned his attention to the sprawling border state of Kentucky, which the Union must control if it was to wage war effectively anywhere between the Alleghenies and the Mississippi. The fact that Kentucky was the native state of both Abraham Lincoln and Jefferson Davis reflected its divisions. By geography Kentucky belonged to the American Northwest; by emotion, Kentucky had strong ties with the South as the first Slave state established under the Federal Constitution. Kentucky followed Maryland's lead and opted for neutrality. This was no more tolerable to the Union than in Maryland's case, but Kentucky was not

*The first foray into Confederate territory: Union troops on a night patrol in the outskirts of Alexandria, Virginia, after the seizure of Arlington Heights (May 24, 1861).*

He created the Army of the Potomac but failed to lead it to early victory: George Brinton McClellan, "The Little Napoleon". McClellan suffered from the general's disease of always being willing to believe that the enemy had more men than was actually the case. And McClellan was a "political general" with his own war aims, which never included the utter defeat of the South — much less, the abolition of slavery.

hemmed in by Union territory; and Lincoln knew that trying to coerce Kentucky with a quick show of force would be fatal. Kentucky would have to be handled with care and patience, and many weeks were to pass before it could be considered that it did not form a threat.

## The Union Takes the Missouri Initiative

Missouri, the third border state, was a different case again. The northernmost of the Slave states and the furthest away from Washington (apart from Texas), Missouri was flanked by Iowa to the north and Illinois to the east. Together with Kentucky on the opposite bank, Missouri commanded the Mississippi, which offered the Union a highway to the heart of the Deep South. Missouri featured a population with roughly the same divided North/South loyalties as Kentucky—yet the Governor, Claiborne Jackson, was determined to carry Missouri into the Confederacy as rapidly as possible. After requesting guns and ammunition from the Confederacy, Jackson planned a rubber-stamp secession convention held under the protection of the Missouri state militia, which he was legally permitted to raise and drill—and which Union forces had no legal right to resist.

Jackson's scheme was ruined by Union officials on the spot who grossly exceeded their authority by the lights of the peacetime Constitution. On May 9, Captain Nathaniel Lyon, commander of the Federal arsenal at St Louis, surrounded Jackson's encamped militia force and captured the lot. This successful counter-coup gave the Union the initiative in Missouri. Lyon was given a skyrocket promotion to Brigadier on May 31, and appointed to command at St Louis with a hasty reinforcement of 10,000 men. Lyon, however, had no intention of sitting back and allowing the discomfited secessionists time to rally. On June 14 he struck again, driving Jackson and his officials out of the state capital, Jefferson City. What had once been the legal government of Missouri was left to wander as refugees, while the machinery of state government passed over to Union control. These rough-house tactics by the Unionists in Missouri—not ordered by Lincoln's Government, but of immense benefit to it—made it impossible for Missouri to achieve an early constitutional secession. The armed struggle in Missouri was far from over, but for the moment the state had been kept in the Union.

While these dramatic events were taking place in Missouri, a fateful decision was taken by the Confederate Government. On May 21—two days before Virginia's secession was formally ratified by popular vote—the first session of the Confederate Congress adjourned. Its last act was to order that the Confederate capital should be shifted from Montgomery to Rich-

*Though stripped of the overhanging blanket of powder smoke, this print, though naive in spirit, nevertheless captures the chaos of lst Bull Run as stiffening Confederate resistance fought the Union advance to a halt.*

mond, Virginia. The move was a tribute to Virginia's supreme importance to the Confederacy, and was certainly designed to render Virginia's allegiance permanent. But it was also a move of breathtaking audacity, for Richmond was less than 100 miles from Washington and closer still to the nearest Union outpost at Fort Monroe. Shifting the capital to Richmond placed it squarely in the firing line, positively inviting direct invasion from the North.

## The First War Hero

The most damaging result of the move to Richmond was its distorting effects on the strategic priorities of the war—Northern as well as Southern. It forced a concentration on eastern Virginia, which became the foremost theater of the war, to the repeated cost of no less crucial areas such as the Mississippi. An immediate example was the way in which the move to Richmond, in May–June 1861, distracted the Confederate Govern-

ment's attention from events in Missouri. As a result the Confederacy was deprived of what could have been an invaluable northwestern bastion against invasion.

The first Union invasion of Virginia began within twenty-four hours of the ratification of secession. On the night of May 23–24, Lincoln ordered eight regiments to cross the Potomac and occupy Arlington Heights and Alexandria. Out in the lead, athirst for glory, was a young militia colonel and the regiment he had raised. This was Colonel Elmer Ellsworth of the New York Fire Zouaves, a regiment recruited from the New York Fire Service and gaudily uniformed—complete with fez—in imitation of the flamboyant French colonial troops. Ellsworth and his men met no organized resistance during their occupation of Alexandria, but the young man nevertheless became the Union's first posthumous war hero. After bounding to the roof of the Marshall House Hotel to cut down the Confederate flag flying there, Ellsworth was killed with a shotgun by the

*How the key Union railroad depot and supply base at Manassas Junction looked in May 1862.*

infuriated proprietor. The affair became the story of the hour in Washington, with Lincoln allowing Ellsworth's body to lie in state in the White House.

The occupation of Alexandria made good headlines, but it only cleared the way for a full-dress advance on Richmond. This would be entrusted to the Washington District commander, Brigadier-General Irvin McDowell. Although McDowell's advance on Richmond was the most important, it was only one of several Union initiatives during May–July 1861, none of which gave the Confederacy any comfort. The first of these moves was Missouri's forceful prevention from secession, but the second gave the North even more grounds for optimism. For this was the revolt of the mountain people of West Virginia, seceding from secession under the protection of the US Army: it was the first defection from the Confederacy, and pushed the northwestern border of Virginia eastward from the Ohio to the Alleghenies.

## McClellan—Commander of Union Might

The West Virginia campaign was opened by Major-General George B. McClellan, at thirty-five one of the coming breed of generals who realized that railways had dramatically changed the art of war. The possession of strategic railways enabled a combatant power to make the quickest, most effective movements of his forces. Commanding the Department of the Ohio from his headquarters at Cincinnati, McClellan knew that the conquest of Virginia must begin with the recovery of the Baltimore & Ohio Railroad. Until this line was recovered from Confederate control, it would be impossible for the Union to shift troops between the Ohio and the Potomac rivers. By clearing the railway from the Ohio end, McClellan also hoped to exploit the known resentment of the West Virginian hillfolk at having been dragged into the Confederacy by the "Tidewater" majority east of the Alleghenies.

His hopes were abundantly fulfilled. By May 30,

advancing up the railway from Wheeling to Grafton, the leading Union troops were hailed with cheers by the West Virginians. On June 3, a small Confederate force was surprised and chased from Philippi, fifteen miles south of Grafton. The Philippi "victory" encouraged the West Virginian Unionists to hold a convention at Wheeling on June 11, nullifying the Ordinance of Secession and repudiating the state government at Richmond. McClellan now ordered a second Union advance up the Great Kanawha Valley by Brigadier-General Jacob D. Cox, while McClellan himself and Brigadier William S. Rosecrans continued the southward advance from Grafton and Philippi. McClellan intended to complete the liberation of Western Virginia and bring his converging forces to Staunton, in the upper Shenandoah Valley.

With many genuine talents, McClellan had two great faults. He had an overweening ambition and self-esteem; his army nickname was "The Little Napoleon," and he liked to deliver ringing proclamations in the Napoleonic style. His second fault was a refusal to move until everything which *he* considered essential had been furnished by his superiors, and to rage at his superiors' frequent inability to oblige—not always from stupidity, but because of demands elsewhere. Thus his advance was not resumed until July 6, but when it came it was most competently handled by McClellan and Rosecrans. Their troops outmaneuvered and outfought the indifferent Confederate force in their path, killing Brigadier Robert S. Garnett at Corrick's Ford on July 13, and moving on to take the town of Beverley. McClellan's successes were hailed with delight in Washington—but within a week the situation had been completely changed by the disaster to General McDowell's army on the road to Richmond, at Bull Run.

## Maneuvering Toward Bull Run

After the move of the Confederate capital to Richmond, Davis took the best steps he could to provide for Virginia's defence. The main line of advance from Washington was blocked at Manassas Junction by Beauregard, the hero of Fort Sumter, with 22,000 men. Defence of the Shenandoah Valley was entrusted to a smaller army of about 12,000 under Brigadier Joseph E. Johnston ("Little Joe," or "The Gamecock"). By the end of June, when McDowell submitted his plan for the clamored-for Union advance on Richmond, both these Confederate armies were in position.

McDowell's plan depended on Joe Johnston being kept fully occupied in the Shenandoah by the 18,000 troops of Major-General Robert Patterson, striking up the Valley from across the Potomac. McDowell himself would lead the main Union "Army of Northeastern Virginia," 35,000 strong, against Beauregard at Manassas Junction. What McDowell never bargained for were such confused War Department orders. These left Patterson with the impression that he must keep his force in being and take no risks, rather than push forward and keep Johnston's men in the Shenandoah at all costs. Patterson's natural caution was reinforced by some brilliant feint maneuvering by Johnston's cavalry commander, Brigadier General J. E. B. ("Jeb") Stuart. The upshot was that Patterson stayed in place, mesmerized by a screen of Confederate outposts; this permitted Johnston to detach four brigades from his army in the Shenandoah and rush them, by road and rail, through Manassas Gap to reinforce Beauregard's army at Bull Run.

## The Battle that Ended an Era

Such was the setting for the First Battle of Bull Run, or Manassas, fought on Sunday, July 21, 1861. The Confederate and Union forces in this, the first major battle of the American Civil War, consisted of raw troops with little or no experience of campaigning in open country. They were also physically unfit, forced marches in full kit having played no part in their sketchy training. McDowell's army took five painful, straggling, undisciplined days to complete the thirty-mile march down the Warrenton Turnpike from Alexandria to Bull Run. With some exceptions—notably the tautly-disciplined 1st Virginia Brigade of Jackson—the troops of Beauregard and Johnston were not much better.

Nor were these the easy-to-distinguish, stereotyped armies of "The Blue and the Gray." The outfits of the rival forces featured a wild motley of costumes, military

*The guns of 1st Bull Run. Sketch of a battery at the foot of Henry House Hill, made by a Confederate officer who witnessed the failure of McDowell's attack.*

*A Confederate Bull Battery previous to the Battle of Bulls Run*

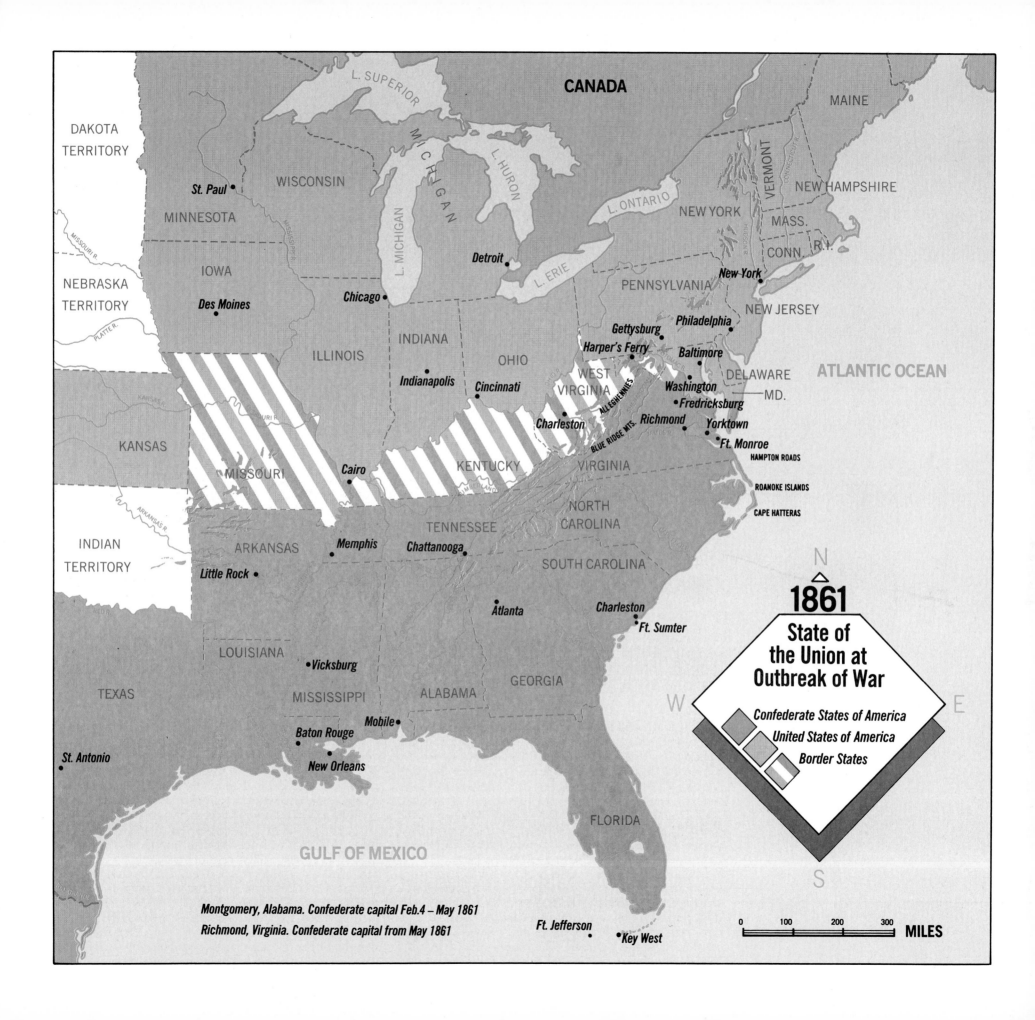

CANADA

DAKOTA
TERRITORY

WISCONSIN

L. SUPERIOR

MAINE

VERMONT

NEW HAMPSHIRE

St. Paul

MINNESOTA

L. MICHIGAN

L. HURON

L. ONTARIO

NEW YORK

MASS.

CONN.

R.I.

NEBRASKA
TERRITORY

IOWA

Des Moines

Detroit

L. ERIE

PENNSYLVANIA

New York

NEW JERSEY

Chicago

INDIANA

OHIO

Gettysburg

Philadelphia

Harper's Ferry

Baltimore

ATLANTIC OCEAN

KANSAS

ILLINOIS

Indianapolis

Cincinnati

WEST
VIRGINIA

DELAWARE

Washington

MD.

MISSOURI

Cairo

KENTUCKY

ALLEGHENIES

Charleston

BLUE RIDGE MTS.

Richmond

Fredericksburg

Yorktown

Ft. Monroe

VIRGINIA

HAMPTON ROADS

ROANOKE ISLANDS

INDIAN
TERRITORY

ARKANSAS

Memphis

Chattanooga

TENNESSEE

NORTH
CAROLINA

CAPE HATTERAS

Little Rock

SOUTH CAROLINA

Atlanta

Charleston

Ft. Sumter

N

1861

State of
the Union at
Outbreak of War

LOUISIANA

Vicksburg

MISSISSIPPI

ALABAMA

GEORGIA

TEXAS

Confederate States of America

W

E

United States of America

Border States

Mobile

Baton Rouge

St. Antonio

New Orleans

FLORIDA

GULF OF MEXICO

S

Montgomery, Alabama. Confederate capital Feb.4 – May 1861

Richmond, Virginia. Confederate capital from May 1861

Ft. Jefferson

Key West

0    100    200    300

MILES

*A moment of defiance after the chaos of defeat. In the aftermath of 1st Bull Run, General McDowell (in profile, center) and his staff pose on the steps of Arlington Mansion, the home of Robert E. Lee.*

and civilian, with plenty of blue and gray on *both* sides. Confusion arising from the difficulty of distinguishing friend from foe was rampant throughout. As for the generals, they were only beginning to learn the technique of commanding bigger armies than had ever before been raised on the American continent. McDowell's army alone was bigger than the one Winfield Scott had directed in the entire Mexican War (a conflict which, by the way, proved virtually useless as experience on which to draw in the Civil War).

In short, Bull Run was fought by generals and troops who had little idea of what real war would be like. It was the first and last battle of the Civil War to which smart civilians—in this case from Washington—would drive out with picnics, expecting to enjoy some vague but stirring open-air pageant. The reality proved shattering. For the civilian as for the soldier, Bull Run was the

battle where illusions died.

Even after Johnston's first brigades joined Beauregard at Bull Run, McDowell still had enough manpower to defeat the combined Confederates. And his plan was excellent: demonstrate in front of the main bridge over Bull Run with one-third of his army, while sending the other two-thirds on a wide encircling march to come in behind the open left flank of the Confederates, rolling them up from north to south. With seasoned troops the plan would probably have worked, but McDowell's leisurely, straggling columns took far too long to get into action. Their approach was spotted, giving Beauregard just enough time to reinforce the Confederate left with two recently-arrived brigades from Johnston's army. Even so, the sheer lumbering weight of the Union attack crumpled the Confederate line, forcing it back to the high ground named for the farmhouse which stood there: the Henry House Hill. By noon, Beauregard and Johnston were desperately trying to rally their men for the defence of the Henry House Hill. If the oncoming Federal troops took it, they would have the entire Confederate army at their mercy.

It was on the Henry House Hill that legend was born, when Brigadier-General Bee stood in his stirrups and yelled to his dissolving brigade "Look! There stands Jackson like a stone wall! Rally behind the Virginians!" Rally they did, then a hand-to-hand struggle swayed back and forth across the plateau. By mid-afternoon the Union advance on Henry House Hill was losing its last vestige of cohesion under a spreading fog of powder smoke, and Confederate resistance was stiffening by the minute. Jackson's stand had won time for Brigadier-General Edmund Kirby Smith to bring another of Johnston's Shenandoah brigades into the fray, after hastening up from the Manassas railway. At around 4.00pm, Kirby Smith's brigade, assisted by Brigadier-General Jubal Early's brigade from Beauregard's right, launched a Confederate counter-attack which recovered the crest of Henry House Hill—and the disorganized Union advance became first a disorganized Union retreat, then a panic-stricken rout.

It was the total humiliation of the Union rout at Bull Run, and the fact that many did not stop running until they reached Washington, which made it seem that the Confederates threw away total victory by their failure to march directly on Washington. But the thing could not be done. The Confederates were exhausted, and hardly less disorganized than the fleeing Union mob. A thirty-mile forced march followed by a battle for the Potomac bridgeheads was simply beyond their strength. Even so, what the amateur soldiers of the South had achieved at Bull Run was more than enough for one July day. They had put to ignominious rout the Union's first attempt to crush the Confederacy by direct invasion. Now it remained to be seen which side would profit most from the lessons of Bull Run: the triumphant Confederacy or the humiliated Union.

*The crisis approaches at 1st Bull Run, July 21 1861. McDowell's flanking advance on Henry House Hill (at right) begins to run out of steam. The 71st New York Regiment halts to trade long-range rifle fire with an Alabama regiment from Bee's brigade, rushed to the scene from Johnston's army.*

# 4 Battle of the Frontiers: 1861-1862

THOUGH THE COMBATANTS could not know it, the Bull Run battle had set the pattern of the war for the next two years: a series of apparent Union successes on all fronts, abruptly overturned by a spectacular Confederate victory.

Before Bull Run, as the first armies were being formed, three future theaters of war had been taking shape. These were the Mississippi theater, which could obviously not become fully active until the situation in Missouri had been resolved; the mountain theater in West Virginia, which had established McClellan as the most successful Union general; and the northeastern Virginia theater—the Washington/Richmond axis.

## The Union Makes Sure of Kentucky and Missouri

Until the demoralized units of McDowell's beaten army had been built up into an aggressive, properly-equipped striking force, any resumed advance on Richmond was out of the question. The aftermath of Bull Run therefore focused attention on the West, and during the eight months after Bull Run the Union gradually strengthened its hold on the upper Mississippi. In these months, the Confederacy failed completely in its muddled bid to gain control of Kentucky and Missouri, and so create a bastion against invasion. By the spring of 1862 another run of heartening Union successes had not only secured Kentucky and Missouri but had begun an advance down the Mississippi, carrying the war into Tennessee.

The best chance of a Confederate success in Missouri vanished in August 1861, when the Confederacy's second victory of the war was squandered. This was the vicious little battle of Wilson's Creek (August 10, 1862). On the orders of Jefferson Davis, Brigadier Ben McCulloch had advanced into southwestern Missouri with 2,200 Arkansan state troops, and a Confederate brigade of 3,200, to link up with the pro-Confederate Missouri state troops of Major-General Stirling Price. These were the troops that had been called up by the former State Governor, Claiborne Jackson, before his overthrow and expulsion by Nathaniel Lyon; they numbered maybe 7,000 effective "troops," with an amazing variety of weapons, ranging from rifles to shotguns. Against this formidable opposition (if nothing more, in numbers alone), Lyon could commit only about 5,400 troops.

Lyon nevertheless decided that he had no choice but to fight. Any other move would hand over the initiative in southwestern Missouri to the Confederates. At Wilson's Creek he tried to tackle the converging Confederate forces of McCulloch and Price by dividing his

*FAR LEFT: Less than three weeks after 1st Bull Run, the war in the west explodes into life with the Battle of Wilson's Creek, Missouri (August 10, 1861). The Union army under Lyons was defeated by Price and McCulloch in a gruelling stand-up fight (which inflicted double the casualties of 1st Bull Run) but was still able to retreat 110 miles to its railhead at Rolla. The first tentative Confederate attempt to break Union control of the border state of Missouri had failed.*

*BELOW: By the summer of 1862, a growing problem for the North was how to treat runaway slaves who came in to the Union lines. Even in wartime, such fugitives from Confederate rule were still private property according to the law of the land. The solution adopted was to class them as "contrabands" of war, feed and clothe them, and use them as labor for the US Army's "dirty jobs".*

own outnumbered army. Robert E. Lee was to do this, get away with it, and win a dazzling victory at Chancellorsville in May 1863, but Lyon was not Lee; he had no Stonewall Jackson to help him, and his troops were not the seasoned veterans Lee commanded at Chancellorsville. As a result Lyon was killed and his army defeated with crushing, twenty-five per cent casualties—well over double the casualty rate at Bull Run, where only 550 Union corpses had been counted after the rout.

Confederate losses were also high, some 1,200 in all, and McCulloch had always been unhappy about the propriety of Confederate troops operating in non-Confederate Missouri; and after briefly occupying Springfield, Missouri, McCulloch marched his troops back into Arkansas. This left Price to soldier on alone—fighting what proved to be a losing battle for the hearts and minds of the Missourians, since a solidly Unionist state administration had taken office in Jefferson City at the end of July.

Major-General John C. Frémont, the Union Commander-in-Chief in Missouri, was therefore left to strengthen the Union's military hold on southeastern Missouri. To command at the vital river junction at Cairo, Illinois, from which any advance along the Mississippi into the Deep South would ultimately begin, Frémont appointed Brigadier Ulysses S. Grant, who took up his duties at Cairo at the end of August.

The immediate sequel to Frémont's build-up at Cairo was the ending of Kentucky's neutrality. Believing that the Union's military occupation of western Kentucky was now imminent, the Confederate commander on the central Mississippi, Major-General Leonidas C. Polk, decided to preempt the maneuver by striking first. Polk, one of Jefferson Davis' most trusted generals—and an Episcopal bishop, too—sent Brigadier-General Gideon J. Pillow across the Tennessee/Kentucky state line on September 3 to occupy the Mississippi heights at Columbus. Polk intended to follow up this move by occupying Paducah, where the Tennessee River enters the Ohio. The Mississippi was blocked by the Confederates, but the Tennessee River still offered an alternative route south. Taking Paducah would prevent this, but Polk was beaten to Paducah by the instant reaction of Grant at Cairo. Grant rounded up every man and gun he could find, packed them on to river boats, and occupied Paducah on September 6.

The Confederate move into Kentucky therefore achieved little other than to seize a strongpoint (Columbus) which could easily be outflanked. The move also ended the delicate question of Kentucky's neutrality—in the Union's favor. The Kentucky state convention condemned Polk's forces as invaders and called on the Union Government for military aid in expelling them. By September 1861, Kentucky had therefore become the base for Union offensives, not only against Tennessee to the south, but for the Mississippi campaign as well.

To hold the line in southern and western Kentucky, Davis now appointed General Albert Sidney Johnston (no relation to Joseph E.). Jefferson Davis had complete trust in Johnston, to whom he had given a full general's commission after his resignation from the Union Army;

but the task Davis now gave Johnston was an impossible one. This was to defend the 300-mile line across Kentucky—from the Cumberland Gap to Columbus on the Mississippi—with a mere 30,000 troops against Union forces twice as strong, and at the same time to take responsibility for Arkansas and Missouri as well.

A. S. Johnston's reaction to this unappetizing new command, which he took up on September 14, was to push small forces forward into Kentucky in the hope that the Unionists could be bluffed into moving slowly. As in Missouri, the Kentucky State Guard had joined the Confederate side and formed the core of a force about 10,000 strong. This force, commanded by Brigadier Simon Bolivar Buckner, was pushed forward to Bowling Green. Buckner's orders were to recruit as many Kentuckians as he could and to patrol aggressively, as though a Confederate advance to the Ohio was imminent.

## The War in Tennessee

Johnston's biggest worry was East Tennessee where, as always in regions with a low slave population, there was

a high proportion of Union loyalists. Like the West Virginians, they represented a genuine threat to the integrity of the Confederacy. The danger would not become acute until Union troops got within reach of East Tennessee, and to postpone this, Brigadier Felix K. Zollicoffer advanced into southeast Kentucky as soon as he heard that Polk had occupied Columbus. Lodged on the Cumberland River, thirty miles inside Kentucky, Zollicoffer therefore held the right of Johnston's line and Polk, at Columbus, the left.

Johnston's delaying tactics were vastly helped by the fact that the Union forces were divided under two commanders. Frémont had his hands full in Missouri, thanks to Price, and could give little effective help to his Union colleague entrusted with the new Kentucky front. This was none other than Robert Anderson, the defender of Fort Sumter—a major-general now, astutely posted to his native Kentucky, but in a wretched state of mental health after the long ordeal of the Sumter siege. Anderson was in no condition to command the drive through Kentucky to liberate East Tennessee, which the Tennessee Unionists were

*ABOVE: Cumberland Gap, the strategic mountain pass from eastern Kentucky into Tennessee. The Union failure to seize the Gap in the autumn of 1861 put paid to the rising of the East Tennessee mountain men against the Confederacy, and added another two exhausting years to the war in the West.*

*FAR LEFT: The South's second-ranking general: Albert Sidney Johnston, Kentucky-born, one of the first full generals appointed by Jefferson Davis. A.S.Johnston's masterly game of bluff in Kentucky delayed the Union advance in the West until the New Year of 1862.*

FAR LEFT: "Drummer boy", by Julian Scott. Boy drummers played an important role on campaign. Apart from sounding the pace for troops on the march, their insistent, rattling "long roll" summoned the men to muster for parade at the start of each day.

LEFT: The pomp of power — H.A.Ogden's painting of the full-dress uniforms worn by a Union Major-General and officers of his staff. The general depicted is U.S.Grant — somewhat ironically, as few officers in either the Union or Confederate armies were less noted for sartorial elegance.

# THE BATTLE OF WILD CAT, OCT. 21st, 1861.—Sketched on the Spot, by Alfred E. Mathews, 31st Regiment, Ohio

1. Rebels under Zollicoffer.
2. Four Companies of the 33d Indiana.
3. 250 Woolford's (Ky.) Cavalry, dismounted.

4. Col. Garrard's men, (Ky.) posted on the cliffs and hill, behind breastworks.
5. Capt. Standart's Artillery, (Ohio,) and the Camp of the 33d Indiana Regiment.

6. 14th Regiment (Ohio) drawn up in line of battle on the Winding Blades Road.
7. 17th Regiment, (Ohio,) were posted on the hill on the extreme right.

### Col. Coburn's Official Report of the Battle at Wild Cat.

ROCKCASTLE HILLS. Camp Wild Cat,
October 22, 1861.

*Gen. Albin Schoepf:* Sir: In pursuance of your orders to take possession of and occupy an eminence a half mile to the east of this camp, I took four companies of the 33d regiment of Indiana Volunteers, at 7 o'clock, on the morning of the 21st instant, and advanced to the position designated.

The command was composed of Capt. McCrea, Company D, Capt. Hauser, Company I, Capt. Hendricks, Company E, and Capt. Dille, Company G, about 350 men. The companies were immediately deployed around the hill as skirmishers. In less than twenty minutes the rebels, who were concealed in the woods around, began firing. At almost the first fire private McFarren, of Company D, was killed. The enemy, in ten minutes after this, appeared in front ot our position to the south, at a distance of half a mile, in the valley. They were in large numbers, and for half an hour passed by an open space in the road and formed in line; very soon they drew near us under cover of a wood which entirely concealed their approach until we were apprised of their immediate presence by the firing of their musketry. At this time we were reinforced by a portion of the Kentucky regiment of cavalry, Col. Woolford commanding, about 250 in number. They immediately formed and took part in the engagement. The firing at this time was very hot, and for a moment this (the Kentucky) regiment wavered and retreated, but was rallied and formed in order and after this fought with spirit.

The enemy engaged was composed of a portion of Gen. Zollicoffer's command, and consisted of two regiments of Tennessee volunteers under Colonels Newman and Bowler. —These regiments charged up the hill upon us, and were met by a galling and deadly fire which scattered them, wounding and killing many. The front of their ranks approached within a few rods of our men, ascending the hill with their caps on their bayonets, declaring they were "Union men" and "all right," at the next moment leveling their guns at us and firing. After a fight of about an hour the enemy retreated, leaving part of their dead and wounded and arms. Our men have found and buried their dead, and taken the wounded to our hospitals. Nineteen corpses have been found up to this time. They carried off their dead and wounded in wagons in numbers greatly exceeding those left behind. It is fair to say that their loss is three hundred.

The gallantry of the 33d was tested thoroughly, and I can say without hesitation that universal cheerfulness, promptness, courage and good sense characterized their action in the fight. I will mention the brave conduct of Captain Hauser, in fighting in company with his men, musket in hand, upon the very brow of the hill, until disabled by a wound, though he continued on the field all day, and did his duty nobly. Captain McCrea with his men held a small breastwork, and did fearful execution among the enemy. Captain Dille was active in rallying and urging on the fight in all parts of the field. Captain Hendricks, with cool and quiet courage, kept his men in their places, and fought without slacking during the engagement. I cannot pass by the active and bold Adjutant Durham, who was wherever duty and danger called him. Lieutenant Maze, of Company D, exhibited remarkable coolness, daring and energy.

About the close of the engagement four companies of the 17th Ohio regiment came upon the hill and formed in line of battle.—Company E, Capt. Fox, Company C, Capt. Haines, Company R, Capt. Rea, and Company H, Capt. Whisson, took their positions with promptness, eager for the fray, under the command of Major Ward. They remained on the field during the day and night, and assisted in fortifying the place. About 2 o'clock P. M. we were again attacked, and at this time Company C, Capt. J. W. Brown, of the 14th Ohio regiment, appeared on the field. —They immediately formed and fired upon the enemy, and this Company, with others, also assisted in making fortifications. Later at night Company G, Capt. Eccles, Company B, Capt. Kirk, of the Ohio 14th, Col. Stedman, reinforced us. At 10 o'clock at night, Lieut. Sypher of Capt. Standart's artillery, came on the hill, and on an alarm fired three rounds; these were the last shots fired. At about 2 o'clock in the morning we heard sounds which betokened a movement of Gen. Zollicoffer's army. It proved to be a retreat. From a prisoner I have ascertained that his command consisted of two Tennessee regiments, two Mississippi and two Alabama regiments, together with a regiment of cavalry and a battery of six pieces of artillery.

The number of our loss is as follows: Company D, 1 killed and 5 wounded; Company I, 1 killed and 10 wounded—3 mortally. Col. Woolford lost 1 killed and 11 wounded. The forces now on the hill are in good spirits and ready for future services.

In conclusion I must commend the coolness, courage and manliness of Col. Woolford, who rendered most valuable assistance to me during the day.

JOHN COBURN,
Col. 33d Reg. Ind. Vol.

urging. As his doctors had warned, Anderson was on the verge of a total breakdown and he was relieved of his command on October 6. A broken man, of whom too much had been demanded, Anderson did not serve again.

## The Rise of Sherman

His replacement, however, did little to transform the Union's prospects on the Kentucky front. This was his former second-in-command, Major-General William T. Sherman. Three years later Sherman would be a name of terror to the Confederacy during his triumphant march across Georgia, but in autumn 1861 he was very different—demoralized and pessimistic, and convinced that the Confederates in Tennessee and Kentucky were twice as strong as they actually were. The real problem was that Sherman was still trying to forget Bull Run, where he had commanded a brigade. The troops Sherman was now commanding at Louisville bore too depressing a resemblance to the raw militiamen who had bolted at Bull Run.

Like Anderson before him, Sherman recoiled from the very thought of a hazardous march across eastern Kentucky, and on through the Cumberland Gap, to support a wildcat uprising. His subordinate in eastern Kentucky, however, Brigadier George H. Thomas, was ready and willing to give it a try. In the last week of October, after delegates from the Tennessee loyalists had obtained Washington's blessing for a supported rising against the Confederacy, Thomas headed south for the Cumberland Gap. By the end of the month, having advanced 100 miles against negligible opposition, Thomas had reached the insignificant town of London, within fifty miles of the Gap itself. Surprisingly, Sherman refused to let him go on. Thomas was recalled to northern Kentucky, where he stood idle, leaving the East Tennessee rising to die unsupported.

Thanks to Sherman's refusal to back this venture, a great chance to discomfort the Confederacy had apparently been thrown away. Sherman, who had astonished the War Department with his wholly unrealistic estimates of the numbers of Union troops required to hold Kentucky—his most recent figure had been 200,000 at the least—was recalled to Washington on November 15. Sherman's successor, Brigadier Don Carlos Buell, also endorsed Anderson's reservations about the East Tennessee venture, and instead stubbornly devoted the first two months of his command to the drilling and training of his forces.

Sherman and Buell could claim some justification for their caution, after a wholly unnecessary Union defeat on November 7. On this day Grant, so far the only Union general in the West beside Lyon to have shown a spark of offensive spirit, had taken 3,200 troops downriver from Cairo to Belmont, on the Mississippi west bank across from Columbus. Grant's orders were to make a demonstration in force, enough to deter Polk from sending reinforcements to Price in Missouri. As it happened, Polk intended doing nothing of the kind. He had no troops to spare for Price, but plenty with which to reinforce the Confederates now being hard-pressed at Belmont. Grant had to fight his way out and return to Cairo with the loss of over 600 men.

It was a dispiriting end to a dispiriting autumn—yet, despite all the failures and missed opportunities, the underlying Union gains were real. Even after the Northern humiliation at Bull Run, the three crucial border states—Maryland, Kentucky, and Missouri—had not joined the Confederacy. Not only had the tide of secession been halted but its creation, the Confederacy, had been shown to have serious local weaknesses—as had also been shown in West Virginia and East Tennessee. More importantly still, time had been won, without abandoning the fight for the border states, to bring into play the North's greatest natural advantage: manpower. When it came to the ultimate military resource, cannon fodder, the North could draw on a combined population of twenty-two million. The population of the Confederacy came to no more than nine million, of which about three and a half million were Negro slaves.

The South's only hope of survival lay in the skill and endurance of its armies: the human tools for convincing the North that the Confederacy was unbeatable. Local Confederate defeats could be countenanced, so long as the beaten army remained in being to fight again; but major defeats followed by long retreats and the abandonment of Confederate territory were a sure-fire recipe for disaster. This being the case, Johnston's game of bluff in southern Kentucky amounted to a vital strategic victory. While the North was mobilizing and equipping its manpower, A. S. Johnston's tactics gained time for the building of artificial defences on the Mississippi, Tennessee, and Cumberland rivers. These defensive concentrations would be the first objectives for the Union armies, when the Northern offensive in the West got under way in the New Year of 1862.

*FAR LEFT: The Battle of Wild Cat or Ball's Bluff (October 21, 1861). Fought on the Virginian bank of the Potomac, 35 miles upstream of Washington, it witnessed the rout and ignominious retreat into Maryland of an incautiously-handled Union brigade — no crushing disaster, but yet another moral-sapping failure by the North.*

*BELOW: U.S.S.Conestoga, one of Grant's gunboats used in the siege of Vicksburg.*

## Debacle in West Virginia

After Bull Run, the Confederacy's record in the West was two crucial strategic defeats—the failures in Missouri and Kentucky—minor tactical successes, and a time-winning strategic victory, the latter flawed only by the failure to block the Cumberland and Tennessee rivers by taking Paducah. In West Virginia, however, the story was one of outright failure, and under no less a general than Robert E. Lee. Lee's first assignment after Bull Run was to take command in West Virginia and eject the Union forces which McClellan had lodged there between May and July. Lee did his best, but everything seemed to be against him. The Confederate troops in West Virginia were in a wretched condition: "hungry, sickly, shivering men," as Lee wrote despondently. Two of his key brigadiers, Henry A. Wise and John B. Floyd, proved unable to work together; the weather that fall was particularly foul, clogging the mountain tracks with mud; and though the weather hampered both sides, the threadbare Confederates naturally came off worse.

There were two main Union groupings in West Virginia: a southern force under Brigadier Jacob Cox, advancing up the Great Kanawha Valley; and the main, central force under Rosecrans, in the Cheat Mountain area. The Confederate counter-offensive, which Lee had been sent to orchestrate, got under way in the last week of August, with a bungled attempt by Wise and Floyd to concentrate against Cox. Their persistent wrangling gave Rosecrans time to march down with the bulk of his force and hammer Floyd's brigade at Carnifex Ferry (September 10). Floyd and Wise then pulled back into the hills west of Lewisburg, each heatedly blaming the other for the setback.

Seeing that Rosecrans was now dangerously stretched, Lee attempted a converging attack on the lone Union brigade left in the Cheat Mountain area. With the veterans Lee would be commanding two years later the plan might have stood a chance, but it was far too ambitious for the raw, dispirited volunteers of September 1861. Some columns got lost, all were late, the Union troops were fully alerted, and Lee wisely cut his losses and withdrew. October therefore came in with the Union grip on central West Virginia not only unbroken but extended further south into the Gourley Valley. Lee now planned to rest and regroup his weary troops. He

*With the Union fleet: the crew of an 11-inch Dalhgren gun (note the massive bottle-shaped swell at the breech built to take the explosive force of the gun's massive charge). US naval fire-power was the key to the capture of the first Confederate coastal forts.*

stoically accepted responsibility for having failed to chase the Yankees out of West Virginia, for which he was generally lambasted by the Confederate Press. Lee took this calmly too, comforting his wife with the reminder that journalists always find it easy to win battles on paper. "I wish they could do so in the field. No one wishes them more success than I do and would be happy to see them have full swing."

### The Role of the Navy

In October, however, Lee was recalled to Richmond and entrusted with a very different task: nothing less than the organization of the Confederacy's entire Atlantic coast against Union invasion. Not content with strangling Confederate trade by naval blockade, Lincoln had begun to play one of the North's strongest cards—the mobility and firepower of the US Navy—in a succession of amphibious attacks on the Confederacy's outlying coastal forts. Such gains would not only provide invaluable bases for Union warships and future landings, but would help sever coastal traffic and troop movements between the Confederacy's seaports. In the dark days after Bull Run, only the US Navy was able to offer the Union a low-risk action of considerable potential value and Cape Hatteras was the first and most obvious target. There the remainder of the former coastline formed a 350-mile-long offshore sand barrier which screened the North Carolinan ports of Elizabeth City, Hertford, Edenton, Plymouth, Washington, and New Berne from the open sea. To secure the main entrance

through this barrier—Hatteras Inlet—the Confederates had built Forts Hatteras and Clark. These forts, then, became the objectives of the Union's first strike from the sea.

On August 26, Flag Officer Silas Stringham sailed for Hatteras Inlet with six warships, two troopships carrying 900 soldiers, plus a steam tug for emergencies and a fast cutter for communication. The warships gave him all the firepower he needed; the big steam frigates *Minnesota* and *Wabash* each carried twenty-eight nine-inch guns. Stringham sailed up to Forts Hatteras and Clark on the morning of the 28th, bombarded them all day and put 300 troops ashore at nightfall. Next morning, when Stringham resumed his bombardment, it was found that Fort Clark had been abandoned in the night and the surrender of Fort Hatteras followed before the morning was out. Here was total victory with only one casualty—a soldier wounded in the hand, by a splinter from one of the warships' shells. Stringham also took 670 prisoners, a quantity of small arms and twenty-four light guns. The news was rushed to Washington and was taken to Lincoln in the middle of the night—whereupon the delighted President jumped out of bed and, in his nightshirt, danced round the room with the Assistant Secretary of the Navy.

With the Hatteras forts repaired and manned with reinforced garrisons, the North decided to launch its next attack against the forts guarding Port Royal Sound, which threaded the network of offshore islands between Savannah, Georgia, and Charleston, South

*Given the overwhelming might of the Union fleet, commerce raiding against merchant ships was the tiny Confederate Navy's most effective ploy. Here the raider CSS* Sumter *(the former US mail packet* Havannah*) captures two federal merchantmen off Gibraltar in 1862.*

FAR LEFT: *Disaster strikes the crew of USS* Niagara's *cutter, venturing too close in shore off the Mississippi delta in November 1861, as a Confederate gunboat scores a direct hit.*

LEFT: *The submarine was a strange new invention used to some effect in the war. This one was designed in 1859 by Lodner D. Phillips of Chicago.*

BELOW: *Always a favorite with journalists and war artists because of their monstrous size: one of the 13-inch mortars carried by Commander Porter's Union gunboat flotilla. But at New Orleans in April 1862, Porter's gunboats failed to silence the Confederate forts after a six-day bombardment, leaving Farragut's fleet to run the gauntlet of Confederate fire.*

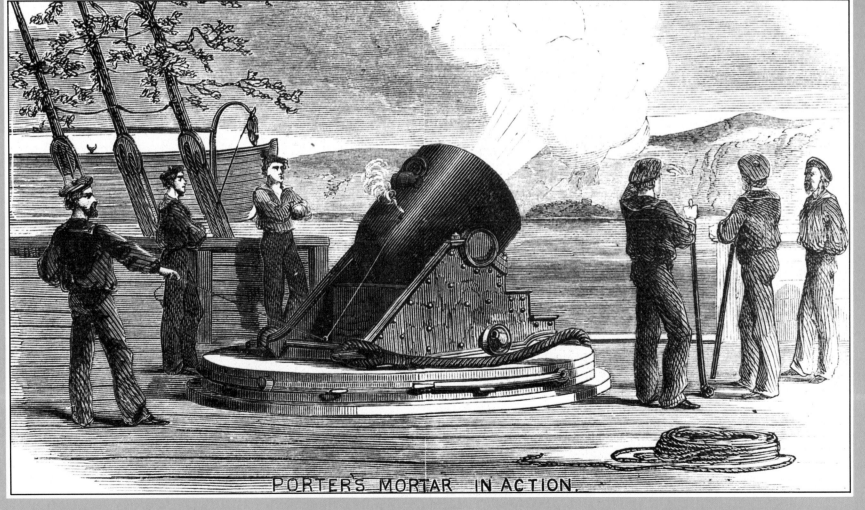

PORTER'S MORTAR IN ACTION.

*The modern, industrialized resources of the US Navy provided one of the many long-term master cards which the North began to play after Bull Run. This is Chief Engineer Benjamin Isherwood, USN (seated, center), with personnel and officers of the Bureau of Steam Engineering.*

Carolina. Port Royal was clearly a tougher nut to crack: it would require a full-dress fleet and an expeditionary force of 12,000 troops. This force could not be assembled until the end of October. Commanded by Flag Officer Samuel Du Pont, with Brigadier-General Thomas W. Sherman in charge of the land operations, it came to be the biggest armada which had ever flown the American flag up to that time—fifty warships and transports, plus twenty-five colliers to supply the steamers.

The fleet sailed for Port Royal on October 29 and

immediately ran into trouble: a gale which sank a troopship with 600 Marines, and a storeship. By November 4, however, Du Pont's fleet had reassembled off Port Royal and headed in to attack on November 7. Du Pont concentrated his heavy firepower on Fort Walker, the most southerly of the two forts defending Port Royal. After brushing aside the flyweight squadron of Confederate river-boats which put in a brief appearance, Du Pont sailed his fleet past Fort Walker on three deliberate passes, throwing such a weight of

*The man whose action brought the United States to the brink of war with Britain: Captain Charles Wilkes of the Union sloop* San Jacinto, *who stopped the British mail steamer* Trent *to arrest Confederate agents Mason and Slidell on November 8, 1861.*

*The incident which raised a fleeting chance of war between the embattled United States and Great Britain. USS San Jacinto halts and boards the British mail steamer* Trent, *carrying the envoys of Jefferson Davis to enlist European support for the Confederacy.*

shell that the garrison fled—imitated in short order by their helpless comrades in Fort Beauregard, across the Sound. Both forts were triumphantly occupied by Sherman's troops, who set about converting Fort Walker into the core of a fortified camp.

The seizure of Port Royal was watched in total impotence by Robert E. Lee, plucked from the wretchedness of West Virginia to command the newly created "Department of South Carolina, Georgia and East Florida." If Sherman had chosen—or been so ordered—the Union forces digging in at Port Royal could have marched clean into Savannah, only thirty miles away. There was nothing to stop them, as the citizens of Savannah knew only too well. If the worst came to the worst, they were prepared to fire their city—"Let the Yankees have smoking ruins to welcome them," as one of them wrote.

## A Missed Opportunity

In the event, Thomas Sherman stayed where he was, and another three years of tragedy were to pass before Savannah fell—to another Sherman, William T. And all this came about because the Port Royal operation had never been seen as a "back door" invasion of the Deep South, merely as the extension of the Union blockade into inshore waters. Though the Deep South was the heartland of the Confederacy, and though South Carolina was the state where the mischief of secession had been born, the Confederacy's heart and brain were located in northern Virginia. In short, Savannah was spared in November 1861 because the Confederate capital had been moved to Richmond in May.

Within a week of the fall of Port Royal, Southern despondency was briefly dispelled by a wild hope from a wholly unexpected direction. On November 8, the Union sloop USS *San Jacinto* stopped and boarded a British mail steamer, *Trent,* bound for Britain from Havana. At gunpoint, on the high seas, the Union boarding party arrested the Confederate agents James Mason and John Slidell, who were traveling to Europe to win diplomatic recognition for the South from the British and French Governments. It has been argued that if a transatlantic telegraph cable had existed in 1861, war between the United States and Britain could well have resulted. As it was at least three weeks were required for diplomatic exchanges between London and Washington and there was time for sober reflection. The "*Trent* Incident" finally closed on Christmas Day, when the US Government stated that the arrest of Mason and Slidell had been unauthorized—an act not requiring the apology demanded by the British—and that the prisoners would therefore "be cheerfully released." The prospect of the Confederacy acquiring the support of the mightiest naval power on the planet had been dispelled.

So ended the year of 1861. The Confederacy was still in being, but already on the defensive. The initiative was held, as it had been for months, by the swelling Union armies to the north. The Confederacy's frontiers had been pushed back from Missouri and Kentucky, breached in West Virginia, and punctured at two crucial points on the Atlantic coast. At one or more of these frontier weak spots, the shooting war would break loose again as the New Year of 1862 began.

*Lincoln's Government reluctantly accepted that the Union could not fight the British as well as the Confederacy; Britain's dying Prince Albert toned down the asperity of the original British protest. The upshot was that James W. Mason (above) and John Slidell (below) were "cheerfully released" by the North after the* Trent *Incident, but not before a Northern artist had made them look like furtive criminals.*

# 5 From Fort Henry to New Orleans: 1862

THE CAMPAIGNS OF 1862 began in eastern Kentucky, and began there because a Confederate general ignored orders and stuck his chin too close to a Union army to be ignored. The resultant chain of events led to the Confederates being forced to withdraw from southern Kentucky and into Tennessee. The war in the West had begun in earnest.

## A Game of Bluff

Since September 1861, A. S. Johnston's game of bluff in Kentucky had succeeded mainly because, as he knew very well, the enemy armies did not believe themselves strong enough to challenge him. Johnston's standing orders to his generals in Kentucky—Polk at Columbus, Buckner at Bowling Green, and Zollicoffer north of the Cumberland Gap—were to maintain Northern fears without actually risking irreplaceable Confederate troops in the field. Unfortunately, at the end of December, Zollicoffer decided to move north of the Cumberland River to make his job of surveillance easier. He was unaware that Thomas, his opposite number in eastern Kentucky, was simultaneously planning an advance to the Cumberland in January.

It took Thomas the first half of January to advance the 100 miles from his base at Lebanon to Logan's Cross Roads, by which time Major-General George B.

*FAR LEFT: Six months after 1st Bull Run: at last, a clear-cut Union victory in the field, the Confederate defeat at Logan's Cross Roads (January 19, 1862).*

*BELOW: William Tecumseh Sherman, whose rise to fame began under Grant in the Shiloh campaign of March–April 1862. At Shiloh, Sherman commanded the Union right-flank division.*

*Fierce hand-to-hand fighting on the outskirts of Fort Donelson (February 14, 1862). Compared with Fort Henry, Donelson turned out to be better sited and better armed, driving off the Union gunboats. Though a surprise attack momentarily pierced Grant's siege lines, Donelson's rapid fall was due primarily to failed nerves on the part of the garrison commanders.*

*Epitomizing the frustration of Confederate hopes in the West by Union "sea power" on the great rivers, Confederate irregulars take vain pot-shots at a prowling Union steamboat on the Mississippi, 1862.*

Crittenden had been sent from Richmond to take command of Zollicoffer's exposed force. Zollicoffer persuaded Crittenden not to withdraw south of the Cumberland, and Crittenden decided that his best chance was to launch a surprise dawn attack on the Union force. Unfortunately for this plan Thomas' men were not, as Crittenden had planned, caught sleeping in their tents. The Confederates lost all surprise in a chaotic night march—just like Lee's attempt to isolate Cheat Mountain in West Virginia. Their demoralization was not helped by the sluicing rain, fatal alike to rapid movement and to the flintlock muskets carried by many of Crittenden's men. The resultant Battle of

Logan's Cross Roads on January 18, 1862, was a disaster for the Confederates. Zollicoffer was killed at the beginning of the action, and his men broke and fled when Thomas attacked. The eastern anchor of A. S. Johnston's frail line in Kentucky had been destroyed.

**The River Battles**

Meanwhile, the Union generals in the West had been under mounting pressure to advance. General Winfield Scott had at last resigned as Commander-in-Chief of the Union Army on November 1, and was replaced not by his own nominee, General Henry W. Halleck, but by George B. McClellan. Halleck was sent to take com-

mand in the West, replacing Frémont, and he cautiously approved of Grant's ideas for exploiting the parallel river highways which led south across Kentucky: the Tennessee and Cumberland rivers. A. S. Johnston had sought to block these rivers by building two forts just south of the Kentucky state line—Fort Henry on the Tennessee and Fort Donelson on the Cumberland River. By the end of January 1862, however, the two forts were neither completed nor fully garrisoned, and Grant seized the opportunity to strike at the right moment.

When it came to waging river warfare, the Union Army in the West had the right tools for the job: ironclad gunboats firing heavy artillery, designed to pound enemy strongpoints while surviving enemy fire. These gunboats were built by one of the North's unsung heroes of the war: the millionaire James B. Eads, who had made a fortune by clearing wrecks from the Mississippi with flat-bottomed salvage craft. The Eads gunboats were available all the more quickly because they were built virtually on the spot, at St Louis and Louisville, and the first was launched on October 12, 1861. Flag Officer Andrew Foote of the US Navy was appointed to command the new flotilla, which not only supported Grant's move up the Tennessee River but proved to be the master-weapons on the rivers.

*Artistic license in this print gives the impression of a maritime disaster, but in fact this was one of the most competently-handled Union amphibious operations of the war. The ships are General Burnside's transports descending on Roanoke Island in February 1862: another triumph for the seaborne might of the North.*

*The Union invasion of Tennessee gets under way: Foote's gunboats bombard Fort Henry (February 6, 1862). Against such an easy target the Union gunners had things all their own way. Fort Henry surrendered to the US Navy before Grant's riverborne infantry had even got into position for their attack.*

**Union Successes—Fort Henry and Fort Donelson**

Halleck, the Union Commander-in-Chief in the West, gave his approval to the plans of Grant and Foote when he learned of the Confederates' reaction to Logan's Cross Roads. With maximum publicity, Beauregard was sent west to take stock of A. S. Johnston's prospects. This, reasoned Halleck and Buell, meant that Confederate reinforcements would shortly be sent to Tennessee, and Halleck thereupon gave Grant the order to move on Fort Henry. On February 6, 1862, two days after Beauregard's arrival at Bowling Green, Grant and

Foote arrived at Fort Henry with four of the new ironclad gunboats and 15,000 troops.

On balance, the ensuing action was Hatteras Inlet and Port Royal all over again. Fort Henry was a low-lying fort, unable to bring plunging fire to bear on the ironclads. For all that the Confederate gunners hit back stoutly while their earthwork defenses crumbled around them, hitting *Cincinnati* thirty-two times and *Carondelet* thirty times. They put a lucky shot through the flanks of *Essex*, blowing up a boiler and sending *Essex* drifting out of the fight with heavy loss of life. In

*Lee's great Lieutenant: "Stonewall" Jackson in his tent. On Jackson, Lee commented: "Such an executive officer the sun never shone on", writing to Jefferson Davis that Jackson was "true, honest and brave; has a single eye to the good of the service, and spares no exertion to accomplish his object". But Chancellorsville was "Stonewall's" last battle.*

little less than an hour, however, eight of the twelve guns in Fort Henry had been knocked out, and the Confederate commander surrendered to Foote while Grant was still sealing off the fort with his troops—a palpable hit for the US Navy.

The fall of Fort Henry laid Tennessee wide open to a Union invasion. The Confederate strongpoint at Columbus was now outflanked from the east, and the outpost at Bowling Green threatened from the west. Johnston now made the hard decision to withdraw every man he could to southern Tennessee, leaving Fort Donelson and the Columbus garrison to block the

Cumberland and Tennessee rivers. As he retreated through Tennessee, Johnston hoped that the Union pursuit would be further delayed by the guns of "Island No. 10," which blocked the Mississippi right on the Kentucky–Tennessee state line. Almost at the outset, however, Johnston's plans were knocked awry by the fall of Fort Donelson.

Having secured Fort Henry, Grant set off overland on the twelve-mile march to Fort Donelson while Foote took the ironclads back down the Tennessee River, picked up reinforcements then came back up the Cumberland River in support of Grant. Fort Donelson

*A Confederate deserter coming into the Federal lines at Munson's Hill, 1861*

ABOVE: *After the fall of Island No. 10, the Mississippi Valley all the way south to Memphis lay open to the Union armies. Here Confederates in the region of Memphis, trying to burn a stock of cotton to prevent its seizure by the hated Yankees, are surprised by Union scouts.*

LEFT: *The supreme penalty: a deserter is shot by firing squad in the Army of the Potomac's camp at Alexandria in the New Year of 1862. Sometimes, however, President Lincoln would intervene. Quashing the death sentence passed on one teenage deserter, Lincoln asked "Why don't we just spank this drummer boy and send him home?"*

*The Battle of Shiloh, April 6, 1862. With their backs perilously close to the Tennessee River, Grant's battered lines of infantry fight desperately to repel the storming Confederate attack.*

was a far tougher proposition than Fort Henry. There were 16,000 Confederates in the garrison, the fort was screened by elaborate trench defences to the landward, and it lay on higher ground, enabling a punishing fire to be laid down on Foote's ironclads. Fortunately for Grant, however, the Confederate commander at Fort Donelson was John B. Floyd, who had helped wreck Lee's West Virginia campaign in the previous September and had been sent west on Lee's recommendation.

The attack on Fort Donelson began disastrously. Foote made the mistake of bringing his ironclads in too close, with the result that three of them were disabled—the *St Louis* was hit fifty-nine times. By the end of the day the Union bombardment had clearly failed and Foote withdrew to avoid further losses. The job was passed on to Grant and his land troops, but before he could tackle the entrenched Confederates Floyd ordered a massed assault on the southern end of Grant's siege line, punching an exit corridor through which the garrison could break out and rejoin Johnston. The attack struck with fury at sunrise on the 15th and broke clean through Grant's right-flank division, but the breakout never came. Floyd sent off an exultant telegram to Johnston, boasting that a decisive victory had been won, then abruptly canceled the breakout plans and ordered his baffled troops back to their trenches. Floyd's nerve had broken, and after dark he abandoned his men, fleeing upriver by boat. With him went Gideon J. Pillow, leaving Simon Bolivar Buckner to sue for terms.

Presented with this wholly unforeseen collapse of the fort, Grant answered with a terse message which gave the world a grim new watchword. "No terms except unconditional and immediate surrender can be accepted. I propose to move immediately upon your works." When Fort Donelson hastily surrendered on the morning of February 16, the North had been given "Unconditional Surrender" Grant to set against "Stonewall" Jackson of the South. Grant was immediately promoted to Major-General by his delighted President.

### War Enters the Deep South

Johnston was horrified by the debacle at Fort Donelson, which had been redeemed only by the last-minute breakout of the cavalry force under Colonel Nathan Bedford Forrest. With Buell advancing at last from Louisville, cautiously following up the Confederate retreat from Bowling Green, Johnston had no hope of keeping the Union Army out of Nashville. There was nothing for it but to abandon the Confederacy's first state capital to Union occupation while the Confederate forces in Tennessee retreated to the Mississippi state line, concentrating for a decisive counter-stroke which might yet retrieve all. The concentration-point to which Johnston now summoned every available Confederate soldier in the Deep South was the fourfold railway junction at Corinth, Mississippi. After the Union occupation of defenceless Nashville on February 22, it was at Corinth that the first great troop concentration by rail in military history took place, in February–March 1862.

By Mississippi steamboat and rail via Memphis, Major-General Braxton Bragg brought in 10,000 troops from Mobile and Pensacola on the Gulf of Mexico; Brigadier Daniel Ruggles led in another 5,000 from New Orleans; from the north came Leonidas Polk with the former garrison of Columbus, Kentucky: approximately 10,000 men more. Johnston himself reached Corinth from the east with the 17,000-strong force which had upheld his bluff for so long at Bowling Green. By the end of March, Johnston had gathered the rudiments of the most powerful Confederate army yet assembled in the Western theater: about 40,000 men all told. Unfortunately time was needed to mold all this

manpower into a balanced and confident striking force, but time was what Johnston did not have. His nightmare was the approaching link-up between Grant, pushing south along the Tennessee River with 40,000 men, and Buell, moving overland from Nashville, with 35,000. Once Grant and Buell joined hands, Johnston would be left with 40,000 men against 75,000—odds which would leave Johnston no option but a continued retreat into Mississippi. Johnston's only hope was to attack and destroy Grant's army, before he could join with Buell.

Before Johnston could put this plan into effect with the bloody encounter at Shiloh in the first week of April, events elsewhere were taking a dramatic turn. Lincoln's insistence that a concerted advance should be made into the Confederacy on all fronts was about to send the reconstructed Army of the Potomac back into Virginia, continue the run of amphibious successes with an attack on New Orleans, and, at the same time, maintain the Mississippi River offensive and the campaign in Tennessee. On a grand scale, this strategy mirrored the dilemma of A. S. Johnston—taking on too much with too little. Lincoln's refusal to concentrate Union efforts into the one theater which had yielded consistent results—the West—was not prompted solely by the deadly lure of Richmond. As President of the

*Massing for A.S.Johnston's counter-blow: Confederate troops rest during the converging march on Corinth, Mississippi in which Johnston concentrated his forces to strike back at Grant, in an offensive intended to win back western Tennessee.*

The coastal grip of the US Navy tightens again. The date is February 8, 1862, as Burnside's three brigades, secure in overwhelming numbers and opposed by the scantiest defenses, storm the Confederate redoubt on Roanoke Island. This heartening Union victory netted over 2,000 Confederate prisoners, 32 guns, 3,000 stands of small arms, and opened the whole area of the Carolina Sounds to Union control.

Union, Lincoln was desperate to win the war by the quickest means possible and he could see no better alternative than a pattern of simultaneous offensives.

So much came back to Lincoln's non-military mentality. By the terms of his office under the Constitution, he was Commander-in-Chief of the Union forces; but he was also a civilian trying to think like a soldier. A soldier turned politician, like Jefferson Davis, would have thought naturally of concentrating his effective strength against the enemy's weakest point, reinforcing success, and marking down the enemy's most vulnerable armies for piecemeal entrapment or defeat. In February–March 1862, the Confederacy had only one fully-concentrated army in the field—Joe Johnston's, shielding Richmond. To permit the formation of another concentrated enemy army in the West, at a time when all was going well for the Union in that theater, was an oversight of utter folly. It did not look that way at the time, of course, and until the Confederate counter-strokes came, in the spring of 1862, the widely separated Union thrusts all seemed to be going well.

On February 7, the Union foothold won at Hatteras Inlet was used as the base from which to ship another expeditionary force to Roanoke Island. Roanoke fell to Brigadier Ambrose E. Burnside on February 8. Twelve days later and 1,500 miles away on the Gulf coast, the US Navy descended on uninhabited Ship Island under Flag Officer David G. Farragut. Ship Island became the scene of another Union build-up, which could have only one objective—New Orleans at the mouth of the Mississippi.

Fort Pillow was held by a Unionist force consisting of Tennessee Whites and black soldiers. After the raid, led by Bedford Forrest of the Confederate Cavalry, there were hair-raising rumors of atrocities, and even charges of an outright massacre. A note of bitterness permeated Northern attitudes after this incident.

*New hope for Lincoln: General Ambrose E. Burnside, who took over the Army of the Potomac from McClellan in November 1862. Burnside was utterly brave, utterly loyal — and utterly unable to change his plan of campaign when his bridging train failed to arrive on time at Fredericksburg.*

## Enter the Ironclads

It was at this point that the hitherto unchallenged range and power of the US Navy was given a traumatic shock. When the Union forces had been forced to evacuate the naval base at Norfolk, Virginia, the powerful steam frigate *Merrimack* had been burned and scuttled. She had not been destroyed below the waterline, however, thus enabling the Confederates to raise her, refurbish her engines, and rebuild her as the world's first fighting ironclad warship. By August 1861, the transformation of *Merrimack* at Norfolk was already well under way.

The first details filtering through to the North were profoundly disturbing. *Merrimack* was being rebuilt with a massive armored shell, with heavy guns firing through armored ports. Relying solely on steam power, she would have no masts, spars or rigging which could be disabled in action. The new monster would almost certainly be able to challenge the Union blockade at Hampton Roads, Virginia, the anchorage under the guns of Fort Monroe at the mouth of the James River. By October 1861, the US Navy had ordered two sail-and-steam ironclads to be built, but these were almost certain to be completed after *Merrimack* was ready for

*The hero of New Orleans: David Glasgow Farragut, the first flag officer in the history of the United States Navy to be rewarded with promotion to the rank of admiral.*

Union troops, massing on the Fort Monroe peninsula for McClellan's spring campaign against Richmond, watch the Virginia/Monitor duel. Though Virginia repeatedly came within range of shellfire from the shore, the frustrated Union gunners had to watch their projectiles rebound harmlessly from the sloped armor of the Confederate ironclad. In this painting the blazing hulk of Congress, Virginia's second victim, is shown sinking at left. In fact she had blown up and sunk the night before.

*RIGHT: As their ship settles in the water after* Virginia's *deadly ramming attack,* Cumberland's *gunners maintain a gallant but wholly unavailing fire at the looming bulk of the Confederate ironclad, in the Battle of Hampton Roads (March 8, 1862).*

*BELOW: Men who opened a new era in naval history: the officers of USS* Monitor *pose proudly, with the battle-scarred turret wall of their ship as a backdrop.*

*For the first time ever, ironclad fights ironclad. The epic duel between CSS* Virginia *(at right) and USS* Monitor *took place on March 9, 1862, the day after* Virginia *had made her unopposed first sortie to ram and sink* Cumberland *and set* Congress *ablaze with shellfire. When* Virginia *sortied again on the 9th to complete the destruction of the Union flotilla blockading the James River, she found* Monitor *(rushed down from New York) waiting to fight her. Here the two ungainly warships batter each other at point-blank range, neither able to do serious damage to the other.*

action. As a stop-gap, the eccentric designer John Ericsson was therefore commissioned to build his own design, which Ericsson had promised could be done in 100 days. The result was USS *Monitor*: diminutive, mastless, and armed with twin eleven-inch guns in a single rotating turret.

Laughed to scorn by traditionalists as "a tin can on a shingle," *Monitor* was beaten into action by twenty-four hours. For on March 8, 1862, *Merrimack* came out at last, flying the "Stars and Bars" as CSS *Virginia*. Erratically driven by her wheezing engines, *Virginia* headed straight for the Union flotilla in Hampton Roads, rammed and sank the helplessly becalmed sail sloop *Cumberland*, then turned on the equally helpless frigate *Congress* and set her ablaze with gunfire. Only the falling tide and the lateness of the day, and the wounding of Captain Franklin Buchanan, prevented *Virginia* from sinking the other three Union warships in Hampton Roads. She headed back to Norfolk, intending to renew the action on the following day. But that evening Ericsson's *Monitor* came steaming into Hampton Roads, and stood guard over the remaining Union warships.

The news of the *Virginia*'s destructive sortie caused consternation in Washington. Unless by some miracle *Monitor* managed to stop her, it seemed that nothing could prevent *Virginia* from breaking the James River blockade, then steaming up the coast to bombard Washington itself. (It was not then realized that *Virginia* was little more than a powered hulk which would almost certainly have foundered if she had ventured out to sea.) But the extraordinary stand-off duel between

*Virginia* and *Monitor* on March 9—the Battle of Hampton Roads—restored the *status quo*. Even when battering each other at point-blank range, neither ironclad could hurt the other. By nightfall it was clear that as long as *Monitor* stayed in Hampton Roads to keep *Virginia* in check, the US Navy blockade of the James would remain intact. The painfully-evolved plan for launching McClellan's Army of the Potomac against the Virginia coast could go ahead, without fear of molestation at sea.

The original plan had been to land the Army of the Potomac at Urbanna, on the southern shore of the Rappahannock River. From Urbanna the army could strike northwest, trapping Joe Johnston's army north of the Rappahannock at Centreville. But this plan was rendered pointless on March 9 by Johnston's evacuation of Centreville and retreat south of the Rappahannock. So the plan was changed. The Army of the Potomac would now land on the Yorktown Peninsula and strike direct for Richmond.

Thus, at the beginning of April 1862, the armies were on the move again. A. S. Johnston was preparing to attack Grant in southern Tennessee, McClellan was preparing for the master-stroke up the Yorktown Peninsula, and Farragut was continuing the build-up on Ship Island for the amphibious descent on New Orleans. To optimists in Washington, the grand design of the general offensive seemed to be moving slowly but surely ahead. There was certainly no indication that three months later the only Union success would be scored at New Orleans, and that the whole course of the war would have been transformed.

*July 19, 1863: Union
infantry charge in a vain
attempt to storm the
Confederate batteries
screening Fort Sumter. Two
ensuing months of costly
siege warfare left Sumter
battered to rubble, but
still — like the city of
Charleston — defiantly in
Confederate hands.*

# 6 Shiloh and the Seven Days: 1862

THE BATTLE OF SHILOH, or Pittsburg Landing, was fought on April 6–7, 1862, and it opened a new phase in the Civil War. It was the first brutal lesson of the cost, in the age of the rifle and explosive shell, of the *decisive battle*—the goal urged on their generals by Abraham Lincoln and Jefferson Davis alike. At Shiloh, for the first time in American history, over 23,000 American soldiers fell in a single battle; and those casualties were suffered because this time there was no early flight or retreat by the beaten side. The armies at Shiloh fought each other to exhaustion. "So help me God," W. T. Sherman would say of Shiloh in later years, when other later battles were discussed, "you boys never had a fiercer fight than we had there."

## The Confederate Offensive

On the Confederate side, the viciousness of the fighting at Shiloh could be explained by the spirit with which A. S. Johnston had enthused his army. This was a battle of revenge: a chance to strike, in force, at an enemy who had been having things his own way for too long. Johnston's ultimate goal was the recovery of all the ground in Tennessee and Kentucky which the Confederacy had lost since January. Nor was this offensive intended to be restricted to east of the Mississippi. Johnston was still Supreme Commander of the Confederate forces in Arkansas and Missouri, and they were included in his plans. Johnston's own attack on Grant on the upper Tennessee River was to be preceded by an offensive in northern Arkansas by the armies of Price and McCulloch, both now under the command of Major-General Earl Van Dorn.

## A Combined Southern Strategy

Few generals, faced with a retreat of unknown duration, have the mental capacity to plan a counter-offensive before they have even begun to withdraw; but this was what A. S. Johnston managed to do in 1862. Van Dorn had visited Johnston at Bowling Green back in January, on his way out to take up his new command. It was agreed that Van Dorn should strike back into southern Missouri, take St Louis and push on into Illinois; this would have the inevitable effect of cutting off all further reinforcement of the Union armies in Tennessee. No less ambitious than Johnston's own planned counter-strike in southern Tennessee, Van Dorn's offensive must also begin by crushing the nearest Union army—the 12,000 men under Brigadier Samuel R. Curtis, who had chased Price and McCulloch out of southern Missouri.

Van Dorn's advance against Curtis began on March 3. Since taking command in January he had done a competent job of recruiting and had built up his army to nearly 15,000 men, including three Indian regiments—two Cherokee and one Creek—an extraordinary recruiting achievement in itself. The Confederate general had a slight advantage in numbers and he was not afraid to use bold tactics, circling round to get behind Curtis and catch him in an enveloping attack. Curtis, however, was not caught out by Van Dorn's tactics. In the nick of time, the Union army was redeployed to stand and fight the hard-fought Battle of Pea Ridge, or

*PREVIOUS PAGE, LEFT: At Shiloh, the Union gunboats* Tyler *and* Lexington *give fire support to Grant's hard-pressed army. Their massive shells did much to halt the Confederate advance by nightfall on April 6.*

*PREVIOUS PAGE, RIGHT: One of the foremost photographers of the war was Alex Gardner. He secured a Federal appointment as Official Photographer of the Army Secret Service, and his photographs were used to recognize and detect spies. This is his photograph of Pauline Cushman, a Confederate spy.*

*FAR LEFT: The Confederate Generals Van Dorn and Price fail to destroy the Unionist force of Brigadier General Samuel R. Curtis at Pea Ridge or Elkhorn Tavern, Arkansas (March 7, 1862). This setback left A.S. Johnston's main Confederate army in the West poised to attack Grant at Shiloh with Grant's communications to the Ohio left unmolested.*

*LEFT AND OVERLEAF: Battlefield memorial and field gun on the Pea Ridge National Battlefield Park.*

Elkhorn Tavern, on March 7, 1862. Losses were roughly even, about 1,300 killed, wounded, and missing on each side; but what mattered at the end of the day was that Curtis' army was still in fighting trim and Van Dorn's was not. Low in ammunition, and having failed to grind Curtis' army to destruction or even to drive it away from the road back into Missouri, Van Dorn had no choice but to order a retreat.

Thus by the time Johnston ordered his army forward from Corinth to attack Grant at Shiloh, he already knew that Van Dorn's venture had failed, and that Union lines of communication between southern Tennessee and the Ohio River were unimpaired. There were ominous similarities between the Confederate march to Shiloh and the Union march to Bull Run in the previous July. Beauregard, Johnston's second-in-command, had devised a plan of attack which involved a swift and silent approach march followed by a surprise attack. He overlooked the fact that the army had never maneuvered as an *army* before and that its troops, though brimful of enthusiasm, had little training in the rigors of the forced march. As a result, the army was unable to deploy for attack on the afternoon of April 5, having ruined Beauregard's schedule by thirty-six hours. It had been a noisy approach, too, with troops repeatedly test-firing their rifles to see if they still

functioned after the heavy rain encountered on the march. Rarely has the approach march to a would-be surprise attack been conducted with so much advertisement.

For all that, Grant was taken by surprise when the Confederate storm broke on him on April 6. Nearly three weeks had passed since his first troops had put ashore at Pittsburg Landing and deployed to cover the Corinth road. He knew that at long last Buell's leading units, after a leisurely advance from Nashville, were less than twenty-four hours away. The real trouble was that Grant had come to believe that Johnston was unwilling to attack—with the result that when he *did* attack on the morning of the 6th, Grant's army was neither safely entrenched nor even standing to arms. It was certainly most loosely deployed, with only two divisions out in front—W. T. Sherman's around Shiloh Church, and Benjamin M. Prentiss' on his left—to take the brunt of the Confederate advance.

The fury of the Confederate assault at first carried all before it, with Johnston's left-flank division driving Sherman into a three-mile retreat. Prentiss, however, gave ground more slowly and finally took his stand along a convenient lane, around which Grant's tortured army bent like a fish-hook. This crucial angle in the Union front remained the target for frenzied Con-

*Not all the war's casualties were the dead and the maimed: Confederate prisoners of war, under guard after capture in the Valley Campaign (May 1862). Their destination would be a camp like Camp Lookout, Maryland, where by the end of the war nearly 20,000 prisoners had been crammed, in filthy conditions, into quarters designed to hold half that number. In the provision-starved South, conditions in the worst Confederate camps like Andersonville, Georgia, were even worse.*

In the holocaust of Shiloh (April 6, 1982), over 23,000 young Americans were shot in a single day. The viciously-fought battle was three times as long as 1st Bull Run. T.C.Lindsay's dramatic painting shows the Union battery at the "hornet's nest", whose heroic defense saved Grant's battered army from being driven clean into the Tennessee River.

federate charges for the rest of the day. If it gave way, Grant's whole army might be driven right into the river. It was while riding forward to organize a fresh assault on this position that Johnston was hit in the leg by a bullet. None of the men who made him comfortable while a surgeon was fetched noticed that an artery had been cut, and within minutes one of the greatest generals of the Confederacy had bled to death.

Even if Johnston had lived, the chance for a crushing victory had already waned. The desperate battering attacks on the "hornets' nest" in the Union center had left the Confederate units more and more disorganized. Grant, in the meantime, was bringing his rearmost divisions up to the fight, while the leading division of Buell's army crossed the river to enter the fray. By holding on at the "hornets' nest" until finally being surrounded at around 5.00pm, Prentiss saved Grant's army from outright defeat; but Prentiss paid for it by going into Confederate captivity with the surviving 2,200 men of his command. As the rest of the Union army fell back, it did so on to the artillery line and supporting front which Grant had contrived. As darkness came down, Beauregard, now in command, pulled back the forward Confederate units and ordered his army to bivouac on the battlefield.

*An early experiment in air reconnaissance. With the balloon held down at treetop level to avoid excessive attention from Confederate gunners, Professor Lowe tries to make sense of the Battle of Fair Oaks from the car of his observation balloon.*

## The Union Rallies

First light on April 7 brought little comfort for Beauregard—merely confirmation that 20,000 men of Buell's army had crossed the river to join Grant during the night. The Union army had regrouped, and shortly after sunrise it advanced to the attack. The Confederates gave ground in good order, but by noon it was obvious to Beauregard that he had no choice other than to order a retreat on Corinth. Both armies had fought each other virtually to a standstill, and Grant never attempted to press forward in pursuit. The appalling casualty list—over 13,000 Union and over 10,000 Confederate casualties—was five times greater than that at Bull Run, in a battle fought three times as long.

Johnston's supreme attempt to recover the initiative had failed and that, for an army which certainly considered itself victorious at Shiloh, amounted to defeat. There would be other counter-offensives, other counter-attacks, other raids deep into Union territory, in the years ahead, but the Shiloh campaign was the last chance the Confederacy would have to avoid being bitten in half down the line of the Mississippi. As if to demonstrate the fact, the evening of April 7 witnessed the surrender of the last Confederate garrison on the central Mississippi: Island No. 10.

## The River Road to New Orleans

Island No. 10 was, from the point of view of the Union advance down the Mississippi, a problem of unique difficulty. The island fortress, commanding the navigable channel with its heavy guns, lay in a deep meander of the Mississippi, between the towns of New Madrid and Tiptonville. It was defended by a well dug-in Confederate force on the east bank, and could only be completely besieged by landing troops to the southward and supporting them with gunboats. The problem was how to get troop transports and gunboats downstream of Island No. 10 without having them blown out of the water in the process.

The Union officers charged by Halleck with taking out Island No. 10 were Major-General John Pope and Flag Officer Foote, who had commanded the gunboats at Forts Henry and Donelson. Pope started competently enough, by capturing New Madrid on March 13 and stationing troops and guns ten miles downstream to fend off any Confederate relief attempt. But Foote had learned the error of his rashness at Fort Donelson (he was still on crutches from a wound taken there) and refused to close in for a close-range bombardment of the island. There was deadlock, until Pope's engineers came up with the idea of cutting a seven-mile canal across the neck of land north of the island, along which troop transports could be floated to emerge on the Mississippi downstream of the fortress.

After three weeks of unremitting labor, the canal was dug and the transport barges passed through it—but they still could not carry Pope's troops across the river, under the fire of the Tiptonville guns, unless at least two gunboats could join them. This was finally accomplished when Commander Henry Walke ran the *Carondelet* past Island No. 10 on the pitch-black night of April 4, under the dramatic highlights of a thunderstorm, with a barge stuffed with hay-bales lashed

alongside to take the worst of the Confederate fire. Once *Carondelet* secured at New Madrid wharf, spattered with the bullet and splinter hits taken by her triumphant passage, Island No. 10 was doomed. Protected by the guns of *Carondelet*, Pope got his infantry across the river on April 5, and the helpless garrison surrendered on the evening of the 7th.

The Union capture of Island No. 10 was a major step forward towards the defeat of the Confederacy. It gave the Union control of the Mississippi from Cairo right down to Fort Pillow, forty-five miles north of Memphis. There was no need to attack Fort Pillow, because it would have to be abandoned to its fate, along with Memphis, as soon as the Confederates had been forced to give up Corinth. Halleck therefore withdrew Pope's troops and gunboats to Cairo and shipped them up the Tennessee River to join Grant at Pittsburg Landing. Once this had been achieved, the US Navy could con-

centrate on opening the lower Mississippi with the capture of New Orleans.

To this end, Flag Officer Farragut had continued with the build-up on Ship Island until, by the middle of April, he had amassed 10,000 troops and a powerful fleet of warships. As Farragut saw it, New Orleans was a far softer target than Island No. 10 had been. The city itself was virtually naked, stripped of troops by the demands of the Tennessee campaign. To block the 100-mile course of the Mississippi downstream of the city, threading out to sea in a splay of deep-water passes, the Confederates relied on the converging fire of two forts, Jackson and St Philip. But Farragut was convinced that this reliance was false. Forts Jackson and St Philip were indeed formidable to any naval force stupid enough to stand still and try to reduce them by bombardment, but the objective was the city of New Orleans itself, not the forts themselves. The faith so obviously placed in

*A significant symptom of McClellan's deliberate "image-making" was the way in which the general's aides aped their chief's posture, turnout, and even his moustache. This is Lieutenant Colonel Albert V. Colburn, aide-de-camp and despatch bearer to McClellan in the Seven Days campaign.*

*Strike from the sea. On the night of April 23–24 1862, Farragut leads the Union fleet upstream past the guns of Forts St. Philip and Jackson, guarding the seaward approach to New Orleans.*
*The gamble paid off.*

RIGHT: *The decision to retain the celebrated detective Allan Pinkerton (seated, with cigar) as intelligence supremo was a disaster for Northern prospects in 1862. His reports, larded with an impressive though frequently inconsequential amount of detail, constantly over-estimated Confederate strengths. The result was to induce a paralyzing caution in Lincoln's generals.*

BELOW: *Pain and exhaustion after brutally primitive surgery: a field hospital at Savage Station during the Seven Days.*

them by the Confederates took no account of the considerable experience amassed by the US Navy in running fleets past forts, and scooping in the prizes that lay waiting beyond.

Farragut's only real worry was the news that the Confederates were frantically building two new ironclads, *Louisiana* and *Mississippi*. If completed in time they would present a deadly threat to his unarmored fleet. On the night of April 24, Farragut decided that he could wait no longer. Leading the line of seventeen warships in his flagship *Hartford*, Farragut headed up the channel to run the gauntlet of the forts. It was a spectacular passage, with the night sky rent by the din and glare of gunfire and explosions—but the fleet never stopped, and only one of Farragut's ships was lost. By dawn on April 24, 1862, Farragut had thirteen warships safely upstream of the helpless forts. He cruised on upstream until the guns of his ships were trained on the New Orleans waterfront. The city surrendered. The Union wedge being hammered down the Mississippi Valley from Cairo had now become a pair of closing

pincers, destined for its final snap at Vicksburg fifteen months later. For his achievement at New Orleans, Farragut was created Rear Admiral, the first officer of the US Navy ever to hold that rank.

### The Great Valley Campaign
By the last week of April, when New Orleans surrendered, there could be no doubt that the crisis-point of the war was approaching. For the past month, McClellan's Army of the Potomac had been undergoing its ponderous transfer to the tip of the Yorktown Peninsula. Magnificently rebuilt from the rubble of Bull Run eight months before, the Army of the Potomac numbered 160,000 men—the strongest single army on the American continent. Now all it had to do was to smash Joe Johnston's army, take Richmond, and end the war. So confident was the Union Secretary of War, Edwin M. Stanton, that the day before the great advance began he ordered the closure of the US Army's recruiting offices.

Yet, three months later, the Army of the Potomac lay

*The last act at Island No.10. After the epic night run of USS* Carondelet *past the guns of the Confederate fortress, a massive Union bombardment silences the guns of the shore batteries to permit the advance of Pope's infantry. The fall of Island No.10 (April 7, 1862) gave the North absolute control of the central Mississippi.*

*After a spectacular passage upstream to New Orleans, Farragut had 13 warships upstream of the helpless forts of St. Philip and Jackson and the defenceless city of New Orleans surrendered to him on April 24.*

*FAR RIGHT: Robert E. Lee with his son, General Curtis Lee (left), after the surrender at Appomattox.*

*RIGHT: Supply base for the Union Army: White House Station, McClellan's base on the Pamunkey River at the outset of the Seven Days battle. Cut off from White house by Lee's storming offensive, McClellan desperately shifted south across the Peninsula to re-establish contact with the US Navy on the James River.*

*BELOW: "Chow time" for crewmen of the Union ironclad Monitor on the James River, 1862, after the historic duel with Virginia. The sun awning atop the circular turret was rigged to keep the sun off the armor, but the temperature inside was always appallingly high.*

crouched on the bank of the James River, battered and beaten after a week's non-stop fighting. Richmond had been saved. And the Union's war aims in the East had come down to the desperate quest for a general—any general—who could beat Robert E. Lee and the Army of Northern Virginia. This rebuff of the Army of the Potomac was the most astonishing reversal of the entire Civil War, and many factors helped bring it about. Most important were the paralyzing attempts by Lincoln and his generals to provide against all eventualities; the eternal tendency of Union generals—McClellan foremost among them—to believe that the Confederates were twice as strong as they actually were; and lastly, the growing awareness, on the Confederate side, of how best to exploit the lay of the land and their enemies' weaknesses.

One of the most obvious Union weaknesses was the strategic sensitivity of the Shenandoah Valley. The Valley was like an infected tooth; whenever the Confederates jabbed it, every Union army in the East jumped. The Valley led down to the Potomac at Harper's Ferry, a natural "backdoor" route for a sudden strike at Washington. Nor could Northern strategists ever forget the importance of Manassas Gap: the side-exit from the Valley through which Joe Johnston's brigades had come to turn the tide at Bull Run. These potential sources of mischief had to be guarded against by the deployment of powerful Union contingents, both in the Valley and outside it, at Manassas. The constant hope of Lincoln and McClellan was that the Valley menace would abate long enough for these forces to join in the main offensive against Richmond. But this hope was repeatedly disappointed by the gadfly activity there of "Stonewall" Jackson.

The process had started in March, as the Army of the Potomac began its piecemeal shift to the Yorktown Peninsula. McClellan ordered Major-General Nathaniel P. Banks to pull his 25,000-strong corps out of the Valley, leaving one division (Brigadier James Shields) to cover Jackson's force of about 5,000. Jackson thereupon did the wholly unexpected thing and at Kernstown on March 23 attacked Shields. Shields put up a surprisingly good fight and drove Jackson off. Seldom has a defeat earned such a rich reward. Banks' corps was returned to the Valley post-haste, a division was taken from McClellan to reinforce Frémont in West Virginia—and McDowell's whole corps, 37,000 strong, was kept at Manassas instead of sailing to reinforce McClellan on the Yorktown Peninsula. But Kernstown was only the prelude to Jackson's amazing "Valley Campaign" of May–June 1862, in which Jackson's "foot cavalry" marched nearly 400 miles in thirty days. In the process they defeated four Union armies (Banks, Frémont, Shields and Milroy)—all with a loss of under 1,000 casualties from an army never stronger than 16,000.

A classic of war in its own right, the "Valley Campaign" was the constant, distracting note in McClellan's ears as he ponderously struggled to clear the Yorktown Peninsula. No sooner had his advance begun than he sat down to besiege Yorktown. With this inaction (April 5–May 5), he handed Joe Johnston a month's respite, complaining all the while to Lincoln that Johnston out-

The immortal Valley Campaign. A gaunt, bearded figure in shabby grey, Stonewall Jackson sits his horse, drinking in the exultant rebel yells as his "foot cavalry" march out to yet another battle. Jackson once described the rebel yell as "the sweetest music I ever heard".

*RIGHT*: *Heavy metal in the Yorktown siege lines: Union heavy mortars, sited to lob heavy shells into the Confederate lines from their sheltered firing points.*

*BELOW*: *Gunners, arbiters of the modern battle — and of its casualty lists. These Union artillerymen are posing by a gun of Battery A, 2nd US Artillery Regiment, on the eve of the Battle of Fair Oaks or Seven Pines (May 31, 1862).*

numbered him, and demanding the return of McDowell's corps. When Yorktown surrendered on May 5, Johnston promptly abandoned his siege line across the Peninsula and fell back to cover Richmond.

## The North Push Toward Richmond

Thus unexpectedly given a clear road out of the Peninsula, McClellan pushed on to West Point and established it as his new base—a sixty-mile advance in ten days. By May 16 he had halted again, at White House on the Richmond & York River Railroad. The main Union army was now a mere twenty-two miles east of Richmond, and McClellan would have been considerably easier in his mind if he could have known of the mounting panic in the Confederate capital. The only crumb of comfort for the Confederates—the continuing exploits of Jackson in the Valley—did not spare Joe Johnston from being urged to launch at least a spoiling attack on the oncoming McClellan. But Johnston was biding his

time. Between his lines and McClellan lay the last natural barrier: the sluggish, swampy Chickahominy River, which McClellan would have to cross before battle could be joined. Until his whole army was safely across, McClellan would be very vulnerable.

On the night of May 30, Johnston's patience was amply rewarded. The weather broke and the Chickahominy flooded, catching McClellan with only two corps across the river. This was precisely what Johnston had been waiting for, and he immediately ordered an attack. To Johnston's fury, misread orders led to a sorry confusion in which the divisions of Major-General Benjamin Huger and General James Longstreet jammed each other by trying to use the same road. Instead of a pulverizing attack on McClellan's two isolated corps, the Battle of Seven Pines (or Fair Oaks) degenerated into precisely the kind of action which no Confederate army could afford: a killing-match on numerically equal terms. The Confederates initially

*Pen-and-wash sketch of a Union charge at Williamsburg (May 5, 1862), as McClellan's army lumbered forward after Johnston's evacuation of the Confederate defense lines across the Yorktown peninsula. The Confederate rearguard successfully disengaged from the clumsy Union attack at Williamsburg, and Johnston continued his retreat to the approaches to Richmond.*

gained ground, only to lose nearly all of it on the second day of the battle, when General Edwin V. Sumner's corps struggled across the Chickahominy and into the fray. As at Shiloh, the aggressive fighting qualities of the troops on both sides was revealed by the casualty lists: about 5,000 on the Union side and 6,000 on the Confederate.

Indecisive though it was for the moment, Seven Pines had three important results. First, it made McClellan dig in where he stood, to make certain of being ready for another such onslaught. Second—again, as at Shiloh—the final outcome did not prevent the morale of the Confederate troops from being vastly raised after long inactivity. Third, and most important, was the serious wounding of Joe Johnston on May 31. As a replacement commander, the army got Robert E. Lee; and the war in the East would never be the same again.

**Lee Takes Command**

The first year of the war had been a frustrating one for Lee. Since March, when Davis had recalled him from the hopeless watching brief on the Atlantic coast, Lee had held the meaningless job of "Controller of Military Operations" under the immediate direction of Davis. In this capacity Lee had been able to do no more than advise—never to direct or command. Now at last he was able to bring his own ideas into play—with the result not only that Richmond survived but that the Civil War lasted another three years.

One of Lee's earliest acts was highly significant: he re-named the army. The Confederate army guarding Richmond became, in the first week of June 1862, the "Army of *Northern* Virginia," the implication being that its natural function was not as a last-ditch defence force under the walls of the capital, but properly as the guardian of the Confederacy's northern frontier. His second move was puzzling, indeed positively depressing; he ordered the army to dig in where it stood—just as McClellan was doing. But the intentions of the two commanders could hardly have been more different. Lee wanted these new fixed defences as a stop-line, in which he could leave a small portion of the army still guarding Richmond while he assaulted McClellan with the larger part.

What Lee proposed to do, when he finally attacked, was to bring "Stonewall" Jackson in from the Shenandoah Valley. This would raise his overall strength to roughly 85,000 men. He would leave 25,000 in the Richmond defences, and with the remaining 60,000 fall on the exposed 30,000 of Brigadier-General Fitz John Porter, the only Union corps left north of the Chickahominy. The Army of Northern Virgina would then continue to attack, each time bringing local superior force against the most exposed elements of McClellan's army. Lee's offensive was not a precipitate affair. It was carefully explored beforehand. On June 12 Lee sent out his cavalry commander, Jeb Stuart, to confirm the deployment of Porter's right and rear. Stuart excelled himself, taking his cavalry on an audacious ride right round McClellan's army—and confirming that there were no concealed forces to prevent the Army of Northern Virginia from severing McClellan's army from its supply lifeline. Then, on June 26, Lee struck.

*The North's enormous superiority in "sinews of war" was epitomized by many military weapons factories. This is the Colt Patent Fire Arms Factory at Hartford, Connecticut, as it looked in the crucial year of 1862. INSET: The Colt six-shot "New Model Army" revolver of 1860 (0.44 caliber) was the most-used handgun of the Civil War. Some 200,000 Colt .44s were manufactured between 1860 and 1873.*

The Battle of the Seven Days—June 26–July 1 1862—was Lee's first great victory with the Army of Northern Virginia, and a brilliant success in that Richmond was freed from the danger of siege or outright conquest. Lee himself was less than satisfied with the outcome. He had wanted not merely to drive McClellan back from Richmond but to destroy him piecemeal, and this he failed to do. Considering that his subordinate generals had never served under Lee in action before, it was hardly surprising that mistakes were made. Jackson, for instance, was twelve hours late on the scene on the first day, enabling the Union forces under Porter to weather a costly frontal attack. Though Lee achieved his superior concentration north of the Chickahominy, this did not succeed in liquidating Porter's corps, which not only resisted superbly but escaped across a "grapevine" bridge to rejoin McClellan on the south bank.

Lee's last major success in the Seven Days was the Battle of Savage Station (June 29), which finally succeeded in battering McClellan off the vital railway link to White House and West Point on the York. But the last two days of the action—Frayser's Farm on June 30 and Malvern Hill on July 1—failed to prevent McClellan from reaching the James River at Harrison's Landing, where the US Navy could support him.

Taking stock, Lee knew that the Army of Northern Virginia could not fight this type of battle indefinitely. Its losses in the Seven Days came to twenty-five per cent of its original strength, of which 3,286 were killed and 15,090 wounded. McClellan's army had suffered less, with only 1,734 killed and 8,062 wounded, but it was also counting 6,053 missing in action, and most of these had been taken prisoner. For all that, the first instinct of Lincoln's War Cabinet was the overriding need to take pressure off McClellan by creating a new Union army in northern Virginia. It was hoped that this new force, working with McClellan, would succeed in trapping Lee—but in August 1862, on the very site of the old Battle of Bull Run, it was Lee who did the trapping.

Though stylized in its execution, this print vividly captures the desperate, last-ditch resistance which saved McClellan's army at Malvern Hill. Though repeatedly defeated during the Seven Days, the Army of the Potomac showed that its greatest problem was leadership, not the willingness to fight.

# 7 From Second Bull Run to Antietam: 1862

THOUGH THERE WERE FEW COMPARISONS between operational conditions in the two theaters, it was natural that Lincoln should invidiously compare the snail-like pace of the Richmond campaign with the sweep and excitement of the Western theater, where clear-cut victories were being won. Even before the crisis of the Seven Days and the defeat of the Peninsula offensive, Lincoln had been taken by the aggressive confidence of General John Pope, the victor of Island No. 10.

## The Command of General Pope

When it came to appointing a commander for the new Army of Virginia, which was to be formed from the dispirited corps that Jackson had trounced in the Shenandoah, Lincoln had no hesitation in passing over Frémont, Banks, and McDowell. He chose Pope, and approved his appointment on June 26. Frémont resigned in protest and was promptly replaced by another "Westerner," Brigadier Franz Sigel, who had fought at Wilson's Creek and Pea Ridge.

Pope did not exactly endear himself to his new command. "I have come to you from the West," he boasted, "where we have always seen the backs of our enemies— from an army whose business it has been to seek the adversary, and beat him when found, whose policy has been attack and not defence." And he went on, ironically enough, to describe the very mistakes which would bring him to disaster in the coming weeks. "I hear constantly of taking strong positions and holding them—of lines of retreat and bases of supplies. Let us discard such ideas. Let us study the probable line of retreat of our opponents, and leave our own to take care of themselves. Let us look before and not behind."

No Union general ever listed a more sure-fire recipe for getting beaten by Robert E. Lee, who found Pope's theories vastly encouraging. Pope's boast that his headquarters would be "In the saddle!" also gave Lee a good laugh—"He has his headquarters where his hindquarters ought to be!" But at no time did Lee dismiss Pope as a complete idiot. From the moment Lee heard of the formation of the new Northern army, he understood precisely what it was for: to trap the Army of Northern Virginia between two fires. After the bruising experience of the Seven Days, Lee knew that given time the Union could train first-class soldiers. He knew too that his next objective must be the disruption of Pope's army, before it could become as formidable as the Army of the Potomac had become under McClellan.

## Lee's Great Second—"Stonewall" Jackson

Lee had also decided on how he would deploy the Army of Northern Virginia in its future campaigns. In Stonewall Jackson, Lee knew that he had a subordinate of rare talent. Jackson's Shenandoah Valley campaign had proved that. After the Seven Days, therefore, Lee reinforced Jackson's division, intending to make it the "ghost corps" of the Army of Northern Virginia, disappearing on wide detours and flank marches, only to reappear precisely when and where needed. Jackson's corps was to be the master-weapon in waging war as Lee wanted it waged: nullifying the superior numbers of the Union armies by catching them where least expected.

PREVIOUS PAGE, LEFT: *The Union advance rolls south from Missouri: Colonel Fitch and the 46th Indiana Volunteers storm the Confederate battery at Fort St Charles on the White River, Arkansas.*

PREVIOUS PAGE, RIGHT: *George Armstrong Custer, at 23 the youngest officer in the Union Army to reach general's rank. Custer's impressive record as a dashing cavalry leader in the last two years of the Civil War was eclipsed after 1865, and his growing desperation to recapture his wartime fame ultimately led him to disaster at Little Big Horn in 1876.*

*The "Summer" mural from the Battle Abbey murals depicting "The Four Seasons of the Confederacy". The Confederacy's last genuine spell of success on all fronts was in the spring of 1863 with Rosecrans halted in Tennessee, Grant frustrated in his advance on Vicksburg, and Lee seemingly invincible in Virginia.*

The Monitor *was rightly famous among the naval men of the Northern fleet. Here, officers pose with a tired but proprietory air on the deck of the great old ship.*

*As the trench lines took shape around the approaches to Richmond, battle-shredded woods yielded ample timber for Union log huts and "corduroy" walkways in the rear areas.*

## Lee vs. Pope

The campaign against Pope got under way in the first two weeks of August, even though Lee was still unsure whether or not McClellan intended renewing his threat against Richmond. Until this uncertainty was resolved, all Lee could do was to use Jackson's reinforced corps in hit-and-run operations from the James River sector, close to Richmond. Pope had meanwhile ordered his three corps, with Banks in the lead, to advance from the Rappahannock to the Rapidan. On August 9, Jackson, with 20,000 men, attacked Banks at Cedar Run. Though Banks fought far better than he had ever done in the Valley, he nevertheless took 2,381 casualties to Jackson's 1,365 and fell back to join the rest of Pope's army at Culpeper Court House, roughly midway between the Rappahannock and the Rapidan.

Meanwhile, on the Union side, a momentous decision had been taken on August 3 by General Halleck—another promotion from the West, appointed General-in-Chief of the armies of the United States on July 11. Halleck decided to abandon the drive on Richmond from the east, and take the Army of the Potomac home by sea. At Aquia Creek on the Potomac, powerful reinforcements would be landed to march west and join Pope. The news that the Army of the Potomac had begun to embark from the James on August 13 confirmed Lee's instinct that Richmond was already out of danger, and he set off to join Jackson and complete the ruin of Pope. Relieved though he was that the threat of McClellan had been removed, Lee also knew that it was only a respite. He still intended to beat Pope and shift the war theater back to northern Virginia, but he would have to

do it before the Army of the Potomac could join hands with Pope. In the event, the nineteen days taken to shift the Army of the Potomac by sea proved decisive. Lee had allowed for ten.

Advancing on August 16, Lee brought the Army of Northern Virginia up to the Rapidan and tried to slip past Pope's left flank on the 18th, hoping for an early encirclement. By a stroke of bad luck—destined, by an extraordinary quirk of fate, to be repeated a month later—a Confederate officer with a copy of Lee's orders was captured, giving the game away. By nightfall on the 19th Pope had retreated behind the Rappahannock and secured its crossings.

Lee had no time to dally on the Rappahannock, for on the 20th the first replacement from the Army of the Potomac—Porter's—landed at Aquia Creek. To induce Pope to retreat from the Rappahannock, Lee sent Jackson on a long flanking march to the northwest, off behind the Bull Run Mountains, as if Jackson was heading once more for Manassas Gap and the Valley. Instead of swinging westward past the town of Salem, though, Jackson swung east; and after a superb march of over fifty miles in forty hours he swept through Thoroughfare Gap and came down like a thunderbolt on Pope's main supply base at Manassas Junction. Jackson's men stayed at Manassas throughout August 27, burning millions of dollars' worth of Union stores and enjoying their first good feed in months. Their role in Lee's plan was now to play the decoy, luring Pope back from the Rappahannock, until Lee and the rest of the Army of Northern Virginia could come up to close the trap.

Lee had taken an enormous gamble by dividing his

*All armies used to depend on local supplies of water to keep going, and units on the march could dissolve into chaos by the straggling of thirsty troops desperate to refill their canteens. An armed guard on wells and supervised distribution helped cut down on such undisciplined (and, in the presence of the enemy, highly dangerous) behaviour. The troops shown here are Northern.*

*Failure of the Confederate attempt to recapture Baton Rouge (August 4, 1862). But the Confederacy's hold on the vital section of the Mississippi from Vicksburg to Port Hudson remained unbroken, and would do so for another 11 months.*

*August 9, 1862: unwonted discomfiture for Stonewall Jackson at Cedar Mountain in the Valley as the Union infantry of Nathaniel P. Banks storm forward, driving back the famous "Stonewall Brigade".*

CANADA

DAKOTA TERRITORY

WISCONSIN

L. SUPERIOR

MICHIGAN

L. HURON

MAINE

VERMONT

NEW HAMPSHIRE

MINNESOTA

L. MICHIGAN

L. ONTARIO

NEW YORK

MASS.

NEBRASKA TERRITORY

IOWA

• Chicago

L. ERIE

PENNSYLVANIA

CONN.

R.I.

• New York

Des Moines

INDIANA

OHIO

NEW JERSEY

• Philadelphia

ILLINOIS

WEST VIRGINIA

Annapolis

DELAWARE

ATLANTIC OCEAN

• Cincinnati

Washington

MD.

Fredricksburg

• St. Louis

Richmond

Yorktown

KANSAS

• Lexington

KENTUCKY

VIRGINIA

Petersburg

Ft. Monroe

MISSOURI

×Wilson's Creek

Ft. Henry

ROANOKE ISLANDS

CAPE HATTERAS

×Pea Ridge

Ft. Donelson

NORTH CAROLINA

INDIAN TERRITORY

Ft. Pillow

TENNESSEE

ARKANSAS

Memphis ×Shiloh

SOUTH CAROLINA

Little Rock

Corinth

1862

The West/East Theaters of War

Atlanta

Ft. Sumter

N

TEXAS

LOUISIANA

• Vicksburg

MISSISSIPPI

ALABAMA

GEORGIA

Ft. Beauregard

PT. ROYAL

W

E

Confederate States of America

United States of America

Boundary East/West

• San Antonio

Baton Rouge

FLORIDA

GULF OF MEXICO

S

Ft. Jefferson •

• Key West

0    100    200    300

MILES

**152**

RIGHT: General James Longstreet, Lee's most trusted and effective subordinate after Jackson's death. Longstreet's corps was railroaded West to reinforce the supreme Confederate effort at Chickamauga, and did not rejoin the Army of Northern Virginia until spring 1864.

RIGHT, TOP: Young Union troops in brand-new uniforms, complete with neat shaves, collar and necktie, on the eve of the 1st Bull Run campaign.

RIGHT, BELOW: On their first breathtaking ride clean round McClellan's army, "Jeb" Stuart's Confederate cavalry troopers surprise and scatter a Union outpost.

army. Apart from the risk of Pope's 75,000 troops getting between Jackson's 24,000 and Lee's 30,000, there was the danger of Jackson being trapped from the northeast by the latest arrivals from McClellan's army. By August 28, however, Pope was on his own: Jackson's descent on Manassas had not only destroyed Pope's supplies but had severed his communications with Washington. Pope's fatal mistake was now to chase after Jackson in the direction of Centreville without leaving a blocking force at Thoroughfare Gap, which Lee and Longstreet, following the track of Jackson's flank march twenty-four hours behind, were now approaching.

Jackson, of course, had not headed for Centreville. He had circled west to conceal his corps in woodland on the western edge of the old Bull Run battlefield, awaiting the moment to show his hand and fix Pope's attention on himself while Lee came up. This Jackson did, with near-perfect timing, on the afternoon of August 28, engaging Pope in a stand-off fire fight known as the Battle of

Groveton. Nightfall on the 28th found Pope's army encamped where it stood, ready to complete the destruction of Jackson on the following day.

## The 2nd Battle of Bull Run

On August 29, 1862, was fought the second Battle of Manassas, or 2nd Battle of Bull Run. It was opened by Pope's attack on Jackson, whose 20,000 effectives held on grimly throughout the morning, inflicting heavy losses, while Lee and Longstreet force-marched their tiring columns up from Thoroughfare Gap. In the afternoon the initiative passed to the Confederates, with the Army of Northern Virginia sweeping into a general attack on Pope's surprised army. As at 1st Bull Run, the fighting naturally became oriented on Henry House Hill, although on this occasion it was the battered Union lines, not the Confederates, who in desperation rallied there. It was a murderous fight, with each army already exhausted by the hard marching of the previous fortnight. Pope's men fought as tenaciously as had McClellan's during the Seven Days. Despite repeated efforts, Longstreet failed to seal off the Bull Run crossings, and as night fell Pope's army painfully retreated to Centreville. Union losses for the fortnight of 2nd Bull Run came to 14,500 killed, wounded and missing; the Army of Northern Virginia lost over 9,000.

*FAR LEFT: A Union propaganda print shows hard-pressed Confederates recoiling from the attack of Pope's army at 2nd Bull Run (August 29, 1862). This happened momentarily during the morning while Jackson's corps took the brunt, but from noon on the 29th to nightfall on the 30th, the boot was on the other foot.*

*BELOW: Modern-day echoes of the guns at Bull Run, in the National Battlefield Park.*

Lee had successfully carried the war back into northern Virginia, but he had always known that the survivors of Pope's army could be quickly reinforced—as indeed they were—with units from the Army of the Potomac. To retain the initiative he had so spectacularly won, Lee now prepared to realize a long-cherished ambition—to take the Army of Northern Virginia across the Potomac into Maryland. Part of Lee's thinking, doubtless, was that a successful campaign in the North would attract support or even intervention from uncommitted European powers. The secessionists had long preached that Europe would sooner or later have to intervene in the conflict; it

simply could not afford to permit the North to shut down the export of raw cotton from the South. A few Southern victories might be enough to make up their minds. In the event, this hope proved spurious. Europe kept a wary eye on the doings in the New World, but for the most part remained determinedly neutral.

Southern propagandists may also have hoped that the taxpayer of the North could be convinced that he was being duped into sustaining an unwinnable war. If a Confederate army could demonstrate its ability to campaign on Union soil and win a decisive battle there, Northern confidence would be shaken to the core. It might even help win the war, for since April 1862 the

*Pathfinders — but with dark army tunics and sober suits banishing the traditional buckskin glamor of the Old West's frontier. These are scouts and guides of the Army of the Potomac, photographed in camp in October 1862.*

How the key Union railroad depot and supply base at Manassas Junction looked on the morning of August 28, after the devastation wrought by Stonewall Jackson's corps on the eve of 2nd Bull Run.

The railroad bridge over ill-fated Bull Run in 1863.

*"Fight for the Standard" (artist unknown) shows a Union cavalryman taking a Confederate cavalry guidon, saber to saber. But until the Union cavalry learned its trade in 1863–64, the boot was more likely to have been on the other foot. Paintings like this had considerable recruiting potential.*

RIGHT: *Another romantic portrayal of the war: "The Soldier's Dream of Home" doubtlessly romanticized because anything was preferable to the wholly unromantic truth.*

BELOW: *Pope's humiliated Union troops retreat over the Stone Bridge; its successful defense on August 30 again robbed Lee's army of a decisive victory over the Army of the Potomac.*

*Ready to march off to the tap of the drum: a company of Union infantry in battle order during the Maryland campaign, September 1862.*

*Blasted by Jackson's guns and riflemen: massed Union dead lie where they fell on the battlefield on Antietam before the whitewashed Dunker Church, itself displaying the scars of conflict.*

Confederacy's fortunes in the West had also taken a startling upturn.

After Shiloh, Beauregard had evacuated Corinth (May 29), because Halleck had concentrated the armies of Grant, Buell and Pope into a host 100,000 strong. Beauregard withdrew fifty miles south to Tupelo, Mississippi, but was then replaced for having given up Corinth without a fight, by Braxton Bragg. The Union tide continued to rise, with Memphis falling on June 6, but then Bragg watched in disbelief as Halleck threw all his advantages away. He split the Union mass at Corinth, ordering Grant to hold western Tennessee while Buell marched east to capture Chattanooga.

the Governor of Ohio had issued a call to arms against the invader. Ohio never was invaded— Smith had only 10,000 men with him in northeast Kentucky—but the uproar along the Ohio had made this extraordinary raid well worthwhile. This reopening of the war in Kentucky, with continuing successes of which even A. S. Johnston had never dreamed, was now to be complemented by Lee's invasion of Maryland.

Not the least of Lee's achievements was the near total chaos into which his Manassas campaign had plunged the Union Army. The speed of Lee's advance, coinciding with the withdrawal of McClellan's army from the James, prevented any clear demarcation between the

*The Union's Commander-in-Chief visits the Union's most important army. President Lincoln, unmistakable in his towering stovepipe hat, flanked by the commanders of the Army of the Potomac after the Antietam battle — only days before he horrified that army by sacking McClellan for his tardiness in pursuing Lee.*

## The Confederates Stride Forward

Bragg's response was to send 16,000 men to reinforce Vicksburg on the Mississippi, thus preventing Vicksburg's capture by either Grant or Farragut, from New Orleans; leave another 16,000 at Tupelo, and ship his remaining 31,000 to Chattanooga by rail, easily forestalling Buell. He then launched a joint foray with Kirby Smith north into Kentucky. This got under way in the second half of August and for several heady weeks carried all before it. By the first week of September, Smith's approach was causing panic in Cincinnati and

commands of Pope and McClellan. As the campaign rushed to its climax in late August, McClellan's divisions found themselves marching straight off the troopships to join Pope. By the first week of September, with Lee poised to invade the North, there was no properly defined Union army to stop him, and a quick decision was essential. Troop morale was vital; there could be no doubt that the men despised Pope as much as they worshipped McClellan. Pope was therefore relieved of his command, and the units of his former army absorbed into the Army of the Potomac under

*RIGHT: A Parrott 30-pounder gun used by both armies.*

*BELOW: The grim aftermath of battle: stretcher parties scour a battlefield by torchlight, retrieving wounded survivors and carrying them off to the horrors of the field hospitals.*

McClellan. This took place on September 3, two days before Lee's first units crossed into Maryland.

Lee's plan for the Maryland campaign was far more audacious than the one used during 2nd Bull Run. Its ultimate goal was battle with the Army of the Potomac, against odds which were positively grotesque: less than 50,000 Confederates against 90,000 Union troops. This was confidence on the grand scale, for Lee had coldly weighed and accepted the odds. He sincerely thought he could win. He planned to bring about this unlikely victory with the same provocative division of his strength as in the advance to 2nd Bull Run, but on a much grander scale. Once into Maryland he would advance to the town of Frederick, turn northwest and pass the South Mountain Ridge at Turner's Gap. Once out of sight beyond South Mountain, the Army of Northern Virginia would briefly split, with Jackson taking off on a forty-mile march back across the Potomac to recover Harper's Ferry on the south bank. When this vital exit route back into Virginia had been secured, the army would concentrate again for the showdown with McClellan.

In devising this plan, Lee was certainly encouraged by the paralyzed caution McClellan had displayed in the Peninsula campaign. Unfortunately, bad luck once again intervened, preventing Lee from ever knowing how McClellan would have reacted. As the Army of Northern Virginia marched from Frederick on September 10, a Confederate officer lost a copy of Lee's entire campaign plan; and three days later this document was in McClellan's hands. Even with this invaluable intelligence, however, McClellan still moved too slowly to catch Lee's army and destroy it. On September 15, while D. H. Hill fought a delaying action at Turner's Gap and Jackson captured Harper's Ferry, Lee coolly deployed the rump of his army west of Antietam Creek, a tributary of the Potomac. Lee had only about 18,000 men in position when McClellan's masses hove into view, but McClellan halted to take stock and deploy his divisions. By giving Lee the whole

*After the turning of the tide on Henry House Hill, Union troops desperately defend their vital line of retreat to Washington.*

Heroic print of George B. McClellan as commander of the Army of the Potomac. For all his faults as a tactician — mercilessly exposed by Lee in the Seven Days campaign — McClellan's enduring achievement was the forging of the Army of the Potomac into a disciplined fighting force, with a morale capable of enduring repeated setbacks.

*Abolitionist print hails Lincoln's proclamation emancipating all slaves on American soil. Published on January 1, 1863, the Emancipation Proclamation was received with dismay by many Northerners, who had never envisaged a war to the death with the South over the slavery issue.*

of the 16th to reassemble his army, McClellan threw away all the opportunities which the chance discovery of Lee's plan had created.

### The Battle of Antietam

When the Army of the Potomac rolled forward to attack on the morning of the 17th, it was in a series of sporadic lunges at the Confederate line; each one intensely dangerous from its sheer weight, but never a concerted smash with all Union corps advancing together. It was another brutal killing match—artillery and massed rifle fire against human courage and endurance. The climax of the battle came at 1.00pm, when Burnside's corps on the Union left finally forced its way across Antietam bridge and imperiled the Confederate right flank. It was now, at the eleventh hour, that A. P. Hill's division, the last to rejoin, came pounding up from Harper's Ferry and straight into action, driving back

Burnside and averting the danger of a Union breakthrough. Nightfall brought a merciful end to the killing, with both armies remaining exhausted where they lay. Lee finally disengaged on the night of September 18, his battle-weary army crossing the Potomac back into Virginia.

This was the Battle of Antietam, or Sharpsburg, September 17, 1862, the bloodiest single-day engagement of the entire Civil War, costing about 12,500 Union killed and wounded and 13,000 Confederate. For Lee, the mere fact that he could extricate as much as seventy-five percent of his army, given all that had gone wrong, must have seemed victory enough. But he had signally failed to destroy McClellan, and the Confederate retreat from Maryland enabled McClellan—and thus Lincoln—to claim a clear-cut Union victory in the field, the first in the eastern theater of war.

### Union Confidence Rises
Certainly no other Union victory ever had the same results as Antietam, for it encouraged Lincoln to take the far-reaching step for which he will always be remembered. This was the Proclamation of Emancipation, declaring all slaves in the United States—including the so-called Confederate States—free men. This changed the whole nature and purpose of the war. Hitherto Lincoln had been quick to disavow, even to dismiss, over-zealous generals who proclaimed slaves free in Union-occupied territory. But after the Emancipation Proclamation was published on January 1, 1863, the world knew that this war was a duel to the death between the American Union and its slave-holding enemies. Never again would it be possible for lukewarm Northerners to pretend that slavery could somehow be retained in a postwar settlement between the states.

### The Emancipation Proclamation
Lincoln had another reason for taking a stand on slavery. The Proclamation was aimed no less at those of his generals who viewed the conflict as a temporary dispute between fellow-countrymen; and that, therefore, excessive zeal in prosecuting the war should be avoided. McClellan was one such, as Lincoln knew perfectly well; McClellan had not only been outspoken in his views but had put them on paper to the Government. McClellan was also known to have political ambitions; in view of those ambitions, his cult-worship in the rank and file of the Army of the Potomac, carefully fostered by McClellan, could be intensely dangerous to the American Union and Constitution. To dispel this danger Lincoln was prepared, if necessary, to get rid of McClellan.

His mind was made up by McClellan's positive refusal to follow Lee's withdrawal after Antietam, claiming that the Army of the Potomac was too exhausted. McClellan did not start across the Potomac in pursuit until the last week of October 1862, and when he did he made no attempt to prevent Lee from blocking the road to Richmond. It was the last straw for the exasperated President. On November 5, 1862, McClellan was relieved of his command, and Major-General Ambrose E. Burnside took over the Army of the Potomac.

*Lee's flimsy Confederate lines repel another blundering Union charge at the Antietam (September 17, 1862). Massed artillery proved a telling counter to the formidable Union advantage in manpower. Veterans of the Antietam would remember the battle as "artillery hell".*

# 8 From Fredericksburg to Chancellorsville: 1862-1863

FOUR CLASSIC VICTORIES—the Seven Days and 2nd Bull Run, Fredericksburg and Chancellorsville, separated by the blood-bath of the Antietam—confirm Robert E. Lee as the most gifted general of the American Civil War. He was indeed the greatest living war asset of the Confederacy. No other general of that unhappy war, and few others in military history, ever displayed such a wide-ranging talent for making bricks without straw. When it came to turning retreat into advance, vulnerability into sudden strength, seemingly inevitable defeat into a situation of dazzling promise, Robert E. Lee stood alone. It was this talent that made Lee the unquestioned master of the Eastern Theater—the man who would have to be defeated on the soil of his beloved Virginia if the Union was to win the war.

## Reasons for Confederate Optimism

Under Lee's hand the Army of Northern Virginia was a master-weapon, marching into military legend with its Commander-in-Chief. Never in the darkest days of the war did Lee ever lose the personal devotion of his army's rank and file. This devotion was nothing like the product of the careful public relations work, handled by staff officers, which McClellan cultivated in the Army of the Potomac; nor did Lee earn it by being sparing with his soldiers' lives. Lee's four victories cost the Army of Northern Virginia 47,449 casualties, the equivalent of an entire Confederate army at any given moment. And if the cost of Antietam is added, the toll comes to 59,859—all suffered between June 1862 and May 1863.

Such was the human cost demanded of the men who fought under Lee. They paid it unstintingly, and would do so to the end, but their continuing savage loss of numbers, whether in victory or defeat, summed up the Confederacy's impossible dilemma. Let the war degenerate into a mere slugging match, and the Confederacy could never hope to win. Each new battle against the big battalions of the North, with its inevitable toll of battle-wise Confederate troops, steadily reduced the fighting capacity of Lee's army.

*FAR LEFT: Building pontoon bridges across the Rappahannock under damaging Confederate fire. Burnside's opening march down to the Rappahannock was well judged, and left Lee wrong-footed — but by the time that the Union bridging trains arrived on the scene, the river crossing at Fredericksburg was hotly contested.*

*BELOW: Union wounded find shelter after the Battle of Chancellorsville in one of the very few buildings left standing in shattered Fredericksburg.*

Even in the aftermath of Antietam, however, the Confederacy still had sound reasons for optimism. The Emancipation Proclamation only confirmed the belief, long held in the South, that the Confederacy was locked in battle with an unprincipled and wholly ruthless foe. There was no such unifying emotion in the North, where feelings were split between doubt as to the wisdom of the Proclamation, and outrage at the very idea of conceding that Negroes were the moral equals of whites. Compounded with the inevitable war-weariness and the numbing lack of any outstanding Union victory, it produced the argument that if the South really was unbeatable in the field, then an ending of hostilities was preferable sooner rather than later.

## A New Strategy in the North

This war-weariness was understandable enough. Twice, in the eighteen months since Sumter, the Union had succumbed to the siren call of "On to Richmond!" Both attempts had been defeated in battle. The second failure had been followed by the first Confederate invasion of the North, and the most terrible battle in American history had resulted only in an unmolested Confederate withdrawal to Virginia. Once again the road to Richmond was blocked by Lee's army which, unless fought and fought again where it stood, could only be expected to seize the initiative and invade the North once more. Lincoln's critics in the North, already appalled by the Emancipation Proclamation, lost even

*FAR LEFT: John A. Elder's portrait of the South's foremost general after Lee himself—Thomas J. "Stonewall" Jackson.*

*BELOW: The emergence of new infantry tactics: a Union sniper, treeborne and camouflaged, with the revolutionary device of a telescopic rifle.*

TOP: *Sashes, swords, spit and polish — officers of the 139th Pennsylvania Regiment on the eve of Fredericksburg. Advancing on the Union left flank, the three brigades of Pennsylvanians led by Major General G. Meade attacked with great dash, and momentarily broke through a weak spot in Stonewall Jackson's corps before being driven back for want of adequate support.*

BELOW: *Confederate dead litter the ground behind the stone wall atop Marye's Heights, core of Lee's defensive battles against the Army of the Potomac in the actions of Fredericksburg and Chancellorsville.*

*A straightforward march across open fields becomes a freezing, exhausting struggle through the mud — all that Burnside's disgusted troops got for their attempt to force a passage across the Rappahannock on January 20, 1863.*

more heart when he sacked McClellan—the general who had built and inspired the Army of the Potomac, and halted Lee's invasion of Maryland.

Burnside, McClellan's successor, got the job for two main reasons. First, utterly loyal and utterly honest, he had firmly stood aside from all the backbiting intrigue and politicking on which McClellan had thrived, and which had infected nearly all McClellan's top generals. Lincoln picked Burnside in the knowledge that he was a "non-political" general, who undertook to get on with fighting Lee. Second, Burnside had led the most successful Union corps at Antietam, pushing Lee's right wing to breaking point before the last-minute arrival of A. P. Hill's men had turned the tide. To avoid a repetition of the succession of understrength attacks which had squandered the Union advantage in manpower at Antietam, Burnside offered a new strategy. He would concentrate the Army of the Potomac into three Grand Divisions—Left, Center, and Right—in order to increase its punch in the attack.

Burnside has been traduced as one of the weakest of the Union generals because of the way he fought the Battle of Fredericksburg (December 13, 1862). The brief Fredericksburg campaign, however, is a fascinating study, showing that Burnside had genuine talents completely lacking in McClellan. What he *did* lack, however, was flexibility and the ability to improvise

when things went wrong—or as the Duke of Wellington had put it, the ability to tie a knot and carry on when something broke. Burnside's campaign plan was sound, and his first move caught Lee by surprise. Burnside did not advance directly on Lee's force at Culpeper, which would allow Jackson to swoop on the Union rear from the Shenandoah Valley. Instead he headed southeast (November 15–17), arriving on the Rappahannock at Falmouth, across from Fredericksburg. This left Lee badly wrong-footed, with half his army at Culpeper and the other half under Jackson in the Valley. For once, the tortoise had outrun the hare, and for two precious days Burnside had an open road to Richmond in front of him. Unfortunately, he could not adjust to the failure of the War Department to provide a bridging train which had been promised. Once it had been broken, Burnside was incapable of tying together the rope of his plan; he could only sit down and wait for a new rope to be provided.

So the unique chance passed. Burnside's army waited on the north bank of the Rappahannock, looking across the river to the heights above Fredericksburg as they gradually filled with the infantry and artillery of Lee's frantically re-deployed army. Burnside had ample heavy artillery with which to keep the Confederates from securing the line of the south bank, but even so his pontoon bridges had to be built under fire when they finally arrived. By this time it was December 11, and

LEFT: Burnside at
Fredericksburg watches his
gunners fail to batter Lee's
army off Marye's Heights.
The Confederate position
was immensely strong, with
its battle line screened from
direct Union artillery fire by
the crest of the high ground.
Far away in Tennessee, Joe
Johnston commented of Lee's
position at Fredericksburg:
"What luck some people
have. Nobody will ever come
to attack me in such a place".

ABOVE: Major-General G.
Meade was bitter at the lack
of support he received during
the Battle of Fredericksburg.
But he was vindicated by his
victory at Gettysburg at the
end of the war.

*The fatal pontoon bridges over the Rappahannock, across which Burnside's Grand Divisions marched to bloody defeat at Fredericksburg on December 13, 1862.*

three wasted weeks had given Lee the chance to lodge the Army of Northern Virginia in a far stronger position than it had occupied on the eve of Antietam.

### The Battle of Fredericksburg

Burnside's murderously ill-fated attack on December 13 sent his Right and Center Grand Divisions (Sumner and Hooker) across 2,000 yards of naked hillside, shredded all the way by massed artillery and rifle fire. The simultaneous shock attack for which Burnside had specifically created the Grand Divisions was unable to take place; the narrowness of the attack front made a massed assault impossible. The result was a series of some fourteen ill-contrived blind lunges, with division after division passing through the mincing machine of Confederate fire. Not a Union soldier got to within 100 yards of the Confederate line. As if to taunt Burnside with the completeness of his failure, the Left Grand Division (Franklin) came within an ace of success. Attacking through thickets and scrubland, the leading division of Major-General George G. Meade found an inexplicable gap in Stonewall Jackson's lines and stormed through. Unfortunately, they were only 4,500 men against Jackson's 35,000; support, when it came,

was too late, and Jackson's counterstroke was merciless. By nightfall Jackson had forced Meade's survivors back to the Rappahannock, where the pursuers in turn were halted by Union artillery.

The grim statistics speak for themselves. In the Battle of Fredericksburg the Army of the Potomac, with 116,683 troops, was fought to a standstill by only about 20,000 of Lee's available 58,500. Union casualties were a horrifying 12,653; Confederate losses came to 5,377. "It is well that war is so terrible," Lee commented, surveying the corpse-strewn hillside, "[otherwise] we should grow too fond of it." This latest Confederate victory at Fredericksburg was not as easy as the casualty lists suggest. Lee had been fooled at the outset of the campaign, and at Fredericksburg he found himself obliged to fight a rigid defensive action with no scope for maneuver. Lee could never be sure that Burnside would not use the vast Union manpower in a flanking attack; and even when it became clear that Burnside was committed to a suicidal frontal attack, Lee was still far from confident of the outcome. "General," he told tough James Longstreet, "they are massing very heavily and will break your line, I'm afraid." To which Longstreet replied, "General, if you

*LEFT: Portent of the new American nation, which neither North nor South had ever envisaged in 1861: black soldiers in their country's uniform.*

*BELOW: The eyes of Lee's army: Jeb Stuart and his cavalry, here seen scouting in the region of Culpeper Court House.*

*RIGHT:*
*Fredericksburg: Burnside vainly gestures at the murderously strong Confederate line, against which the Union Grand Divisions had marched to ruin. "Oh, those men! Those men!" he was heard to lament, "I am thinking of them all the time".*

*FAR RIGHT: "Grant and his Generals, 1864" — after nearly three years of agonizing trial-and-error, Abraham Lincoln had found his war-winning team at last. To the jealous voices who had pressed for Grant's replacement, Lincoln had retorted "I can't spare this man: he fights".*

RIGHT: *The dismal face of life in winter quarters, 1863. This is the Provost Marshal (military police) headquarters at Aquia Creek, Burnside's main supply base on the Potomac River.*

BELOW: *A portrait group of the US Navy's top three admirals. From left to right: Samuel F. Du Pont, David G. Farragut, and David D. Porter.*

put every man on the other side of the Potomac on that field to approach me over the same line, and give me plenty of ammunition, I will kill them all before they reach my line." There were not many occasions when Robert E. Lee needed cheering up by his subordinates, but Fredericksburg was one of them. For having shaken Lee as never before, Burnside deserves more credit than he has usually been given.

## A Confederate Victory Without Triumph

Moreover, Fredericksburg was a victory which Lee was wholly unable to exploit. Burnside, agonizing over his losses and accepting all responsibility for his defeat, withdrew the Army of the Potomac to the north bank of the Rappahannock. Even so, Burnside did not despair. He was determined to keep the initiative, exploiting his still impressive numerical superiority over Lee. For his part, Lee had to accept that the victorious Army of Northern Virginia must stay on the defensive. Unlike Burnside, Lee did not have bridging trains to cope with flooding rivers, or engineers to restore dissolving roads. Even after the thousands of Union corpses on the Fredericksburg battlefield had been stripped for clothing and footwear, Lee's army remained threadbare. One of Jackson's brigades had 400 barefoot men out of 1,500. If Burnside kept up the pressure, Lee would be in trouble, but Burnside was prevented from doing so, as much by the rampant disloyalty of his corps commanders as by the appalling winter weather. With Hooker, Franklin, and Sumner freely stating their opinion that Burnside must go, Burnside's position had become virtually impossible by mid-January 1863. His

*Time after time, Grant saw his gunboat flotillas blocked and ambushed amid the swampy and treacherous inlets of the Mississippi bayous.*

PREVIOUS PAGE: Winslow Homer's "A Rainy Day in Camp" — Union troops make themselves as comfortable as they can amid the dreariness of winter quarters.

ABOVE: The steamboat Clinch, pressed into service as a Union troop transport for the Western "river war". It was in an improvised fleet of such vessels that U.S. Grant took the vital first trick by occupying Paducah in September 1861. This enabled Grant to push his flotillas up first the Tennessee River, then the Cumberland River (January-February 1862), sealing the fate of Forts Henry and Donelson.

RIGHT: Portrait of a Confederate blockade-runner: the paddle-wheeler Lady Sterling, of Wilmington, North Carolina. After an eventful career dodging the cruisers of the US Navy she was eventually captured, pressed into Union service, and ended the war as USS Hornet.

attempt to move upstream and cross the upper Rappahannock behind Lee's left foundered in liquid mud on January 20. Burnside thereupon offered Lincoln a straight choice: either sack the trouble-making corps commanders or accept Burnside's own resignation.

## The Union Setbacks

Lincoln reluctantly decided to accept Burnside's resignation. He could not countenance a purge of the Army of the Potomac—the news from the other fronts was too uniformly bad. On the Mississippi, Grant's first drive on Vicksburg had been stopped in its tracks on December 29 at Chickasaw Bluff. Hard-riding Confederate cavalry, capturing Grant's supply base at Holly Springs a week earlier, had left Grant with no option but to try to take Vicksburg with what he had. At Chickasaw Bluff, Lieutenant-General John Pemberton, commanding the Vicksburg sector, drove back Sherman, suffering over 1,700 casualties. Grant withdrew to build up a new base at Milliken's Bend, twenty miles north of Vicksburg

and on the wrong—west—bank of the river. By the New Year of 1863 it was clear that there would be no more runaway Union victories on the Mississippi, and that the campaign against Vicksburg would be long and hard. Even so, Lincoln refused point-blank to replace Grant. "I can't spare this man," was his terse comment; "he fights."

The news was equally dismaying from central Tennessee. On December 26, Rosecrans marched out of Nashville to attack Bragg's army at Murfreesboro and drive on to Chattanooga, 125 miles to the southeast. But on December 31, 1862, Bragg struck first, staging an uncanny replay of Shiloh by unleashing a storming attack on Rosecrans in the Battle of Stone's River, or Murfreesboro. As at Shiloh, the attacking Confederates bent the tortured Union army into a horseshoe before its desperate resistance took effect. Repeated Confederate assaults only increased the toll in casualties, without finishing the job of routing "Old Rosey's" men. The cost of Murfreesboro was proportionately worse than that of

*Exported cargoes of Confederate cotton which managed to run the Union blockade were few and far between, but those which did get through made fortunes for their owners. One such cotton cargo is shown on the quayside at Nassau, New Providence, in 1864.*

Fredericksburg; Rosecrans, with an army one-third the size of Burnside's, lost the same number of men (nearly 13,000). But Bragg's losses came to over 10,000, and the subsequent Union refusal to retreat on Nashville left Bragg with no option but to retreat himself, abandoning Murfreesboro to Rosecrans' exhausted army. The withdrawal of Bragg enabled Lincoln to claim the battle as a victory, but it was a victory in name only. Nearly six months were to pass before Rosecrans felt himself ready to take the offensive again.

And so it was that with the Union war effort fought to a standstill on the Mississippi and in Tennessee, Lincoln shrank from the prospect of purging the high command of the Army of the Potomac. He therefore accepted Burnside's resignation and made one of the most extraordinary appointments in modern military history. To "Fighting Joe" Hooker, the most outspoken and disloyal of Burnside's generals, Lincoln wrote a devastating letter of rebuke—and at the same time appointed Hooker to command. Lincoln poured scorn on Hooker's assertions, previously expressed, that both the army and the Government needed a dictator. "Only those generals who gain successes can set up dictators,"

wrote Lincoln. "What I now ask of you is military success and I will risk the dictatorship." And he ended, "Beware of rashness, but with energy and sleepless vigilance go forward and give us victories."

### North and South Take Stock: Winter 1863

An unusually foul North Virginian winter enforced a virtual two months' truce, in which Lee and Hooker did all they could to prepare their armies for the spring campaign. As ever, the North had all the material advantages, and Hooker made admirable use of them. Like McClellan, he was a good organizer, and the soaring morale of the Army of the Potomac meant that the inevitable cult of personality encouraged by Hooker was a small price to pay. It was certainly outweighed by a long-overdue reform. This was Hooker's amalgamation of the Union cavalry into a unified cavalry corps, able to take on "Jeb" Stuart's redoubtable cavalry division. Hooker also abolished Burnside's Grand Divisions, in order to have more flexibility in the attack. By the last week of April 1863, Hooker had built up the Army of the Potomac to a greater-than-ever strength of 130,000, proclaiming that it was "the finest army on the

planet." Radiating the confidence which he had certainly infused into his army, Hooker boasted: "My plans are perfect. May God have mercy on General Lee, for I will have none!"

Lee was far less sanguine. He had had to send Longstreet's corps to the lower James River at the end of February to cover the Union forces holding Norfolk, Virginia—the only lasting Northern gain from the Peninsula campaign of summer 1862. The continuing supply crisis of the Army of Northern Virginia meant that Longstreet had to act as forager and food-collector on the lower James. By the end of April he still had not rejoined Lee. This left Lee with barely 60,000 effectives to hold the Rappahannock at, and upstream of, Fredericksburg, in the knowledge that Hooker had over twice his numbers. He was also aware that Hooker had ample resources with which to flank and crush the truncated Confederate army. By nightfall on April 30, Hooker's VI Corps, with 47,000 men, was facing Lee

from across the river at Fredericksburg. Concentrating behind Lee's left flank at Chancellorsville, nine miles west of Fredericksburg, Hooker was amassing the bulk of his army, 72,000 strong. Between these two fires, Lee's chances of escape seemed non-existent.

## Chancellorsville: A Confederate Legend

Hooker's "perfect" planning, however, was based on the fatal premise that Lee would react the way Hooker wanted him to. Hooker had opened the campaign by sending the new Union cavalry corps rampaging south behind Lee's rear. This was supposed to lure away Stuart's cavalry, blinding Lee to the stealthy closing of Hooker's trap; instead, Stuart stayed with Lee, and correctly located the main Union force as coming from Chancellorsville. Armed with this information, Lee did the wholly unexpected thing. In the face of overwhelming odds he divided his army and, leaving 10,000 men to hold the heights above Fredericksburg, turned

*ABOVE: The gloomy woodlands of the Wilderness, through which Stonewall Jackson's yelling furies came storming to ruin Hooker's hopes and complete Lee's "perfect victory" at Chancellorsville.*

*FAR LEFT: Union soldiers overlook their camp. Whether encamped or on the march, the sheer size and organization of the Army of the Potomac was always impressive.*

west to face Hooker with the remaining 42,000. When Hooker resumed the advance from Chancellorsville on the morning of May 1, his leading units ran straight into spirited Confederate fire where no Confederates should have been.

Fatally nonplussed by this turn of events, Hooker changed his plan. He ordered a withdrawal to Chancellorsville, there to stand on the defensive and do to Lee what Lee had done to Burnside at Fredericksburg. "I have got Lee just where I want him," Hooker reassured his baffled corps commanders; "he must fight me on my own ground." With these words, the battle which Hooker could not lose became—in his own mind—the battle which Lee could not win. He had abandoned the initiative to Lee.

For the rest of the strange respite thus handed to him on May 1, Lee knew that he was still in deadly peril. It was now that he took the most audacious decision of his career. After a tense consultation with Stonewall Jackson, Lee decided to divide his army yet again. He would continue to fix Hooker's attention—with 14,000 men against 70,000. Jackson meanwhile would lead the remaining 28,000 on a deep flank march, southwest and then north to where the Union right flank hung "in the air," three miles west of Chancellorsville. It would take Jackson nearly the whole of May 2 to get into position,

*LEFT: Jackson's battle line erupts from the woods, hurling the Union right flank into confusion and turning the tide at Chancellorsville.*

*BELOW: For once, Farragut's aggression was no match for the natural strength of the Confederate defenses and only two of his seven ships forced their way past the Confederate forts to win safety upstream prior to the Vicksburg campaign. But at least he had seen to it that Port Hudson would be unable to send any effective help to the Vicksburg garrison.*

during which time Lee could only pray that Hooker would not guess what was afoot. If Hooker resumed his attack on May 2, Lee's tiny force would surely be crushed.

Jackson's flank march got under way early on the morning of May 2. It was spotted, but Hooker decided that the mysterious Confederate units were merely the start of Lee's retreat. All he did was to send the corps of Major-General Dan E. Sickles to pursue. Jackson easily held off Sickles with his rearmost brigade, while at the same time hounding the rest of his force on its way. They arrived on schedule, poised above Hooker's naked right flank, at sunset on May 2.

The rest is legend: how Jackson's men tore exultingly through the panicking Union lines, ripping open the Union right flank, and battering their way back eastward to rejoin Lee. But it was Jackson who saw the supreme opportunity—the chance of striking north to seize the main ford over the Rappahannock, sealing off Hooker's line of retreat and trapping the whole Union army. Heedless of the dangerous confusion into which his own forces had fallen during their attack, Jackson pressed forward in the darkness, rode in front of North Carolina troops on the lookout for Yankee cavalry—and fell, shot from his horse by his own men. As Jackson was carried to the rear, mortally wounded, the supreme opportunity passed. He had not had time to tell his subordinates what he had in mind, and Jeb Stuart, taking command of the flank force, concentrated on rejoining Lee.

Daybreak on May 3 found Hooker's army with its right flank in tatters, but still with 70,000 men between the divisions of Lee's force. The sheer shock of Jackson's attack had completely demoralized Hooker. Being momentarily stunned by a near-miss from a Confederate cannon ball only sharpened his determination to get the army safely back across the Rappahannock. Lee meanwhile faced about to force Hooker's VI Corps out of their positions west of Fredericksburg, dividing his forces again—for the third time—to do it. By nightfall on May 4, 1863, Hooker's "perfect" plan lay in perfect ruins.

The Battle of Chancellorsville, May 2–4, 1863, is remembered as Lee's most dazzling victory, in which 60,000 Confederates drove back 130,000 Union troops. And, indeed, Chancellorsville was a superb achievement of the military art, but the price paid was heavy: the death of Jackson, from his wounds, on May 10. Not only did Chancellorsville end the magic partnership of Lee and Jackson, but it left Richmond as vulnerable as it had been a year before, on the eve of the Seven Days. Once the battered Army of the Potomac had pulled itself together, Lee knew only too well that a renewed drive on Richmond would be hard to hold.

After Chancellorsville, therefore, Lee decided on a second campaign north of the Potomac, not in Maryland this time but further north, in Pennsylvania, threatening the nearest war factories of the North. By the end of May, with Longstreet's corps retrieved from the lower James River, the Army of Northern Virginia had been restored to a strength of 75,000 men. On June 3 it set out again on the road north—the road to a town called Gettysburg.

*Bragg's Confederates beat in vain against Rosecrans' tortured battle line at Murfreesboro or Stone's River (December 31, 1862).*

A moment of disaster for Southern hopes: Jackson reels in the saddle, shot by his own men at Chancellorsville. His left arm had to be amputated just below the shoulder, and though Jackson's immediate recovery was good, he went into a rapid decline — dying of pneumonia four days after the battle.

# 9 Gettysburg and Vicksburg: 1863

I

T IS EASY TO POINT to Chancellorsville as the lowest point reached by Union fortunes in the Civil War—easy, but wrong. True, the Union was still no nearer to seizing the tantalizing prize of the Confederate capital than it had been, but the real nadir had come two years earlier, in July 1861, with the fiasco of 1st Bull Run. At that date the Confederacy's frontiers had still been virtually intact. By the time of Chancellorsville, twenty-two months later, however, the Union's position was far stronger. Its vast resources had been mobilized; the frontier states had been saved for the Union; and the Union armies were lodged in northern Virginia, central Tennessee, and the lower Mississippi. The Confederate hold on the Mississippi River had been reduced to a mere 150-mile stretch from Vicksburg downstream to Port Hudson.

## Defeatist Moves in the North
The two months after Chancellorsville dispelled the last illusions that the South was unbeatable—the illusions which, after Fredericksburg, had threatened to produce an active political "peace party" in the North.

*PREVIOUS PAGE, LEFT:*
*Pathetic attempts to help the*
*wounded and dying who lay*
*in their thousands across the*
*fields at Gettysburg.*

*PREVIOUS PAGE, TOP RIGHT:*
*With the US Navy: Divine*
*Service aboard USS* Passaic
*during the weary months of*
*blockade duties off*
*Charleston, South Carolina.*

*PREVIOUS PAGE, BOTTOM*
*RIGHT: The world's first*
*naval action fought by*
*seagoing ironclads: Du*
*Pont's flagship* New
Ironsides, *supported by two*
*turret ironclads, bombards*
*Fort Sumter on April 7,*
*1863.*

*RIGHT: Curtain-raiser to the*
*Vicksburg campaign:*
*Farragut's fleet runs the*
*gauntlet of the Port Hudson*
*forts, March 14, 1863.*

These pessimists were drawn from the ranks of the Northern Democrats. Left leaderless since the death of Stephen Douglas from typhoid in June 1861, they had found a leader in Ohio Congressman Clement L. Vallandigham, who denounced the Emancipation Proclamation as the latest of the President's myriad errors. Vallandigham and his fellow "Copperheads" (named by their enemies for the poisonous snake of that name) pressed for a cessation of hostilities as the only way in which the South could ever be brought back into the Union. The Copperheads never mounted a serious political threat to Lincoln's administration, and their influence waned with the mounting optimism for Hooker's spring campaign. Nor did they get a chance to make capital out of the Chancellorsville fiasco, for on May 5 Vallandigham was arrested. This was carried out on the orders of General Burnside, now commanding the Department of the Ohio. Burnside ordered Vallandigham to be imprisoned for the duration of the war; Lincoln commuted the sentence into an exile to the Confederacy. This was a neat move, for Vallandigham was made thoroughly unwelcome in the South and soon departed, running the Union blockade, for Canada. In the event, any embarrassment caused by the Copperheads was obviated by the stunning events of May–July 1863—the months of Gettysburg and Vicksburg.

## The Build-up to Vicksburg

In the month after Chancellorsville, Lee's most urgent concern was to argue Jefferson Davis out of detaching Longstreet's corps from the Army of Northern Virginia, and sending it to Mississippi to assist in the defense of Vicksburg. From January to April 1863, undeterred by his failure at Chickasaw Bluff in December, Grant had tried ceaselessly to lodge his army on the Mississippi east bank, thus cutting off the landward approaches to Vicksburg. The problem here was that the immensely long overland line of march from his rear base at Memphis was wide open to Confederate cavalry raids. Grant therefore spent the first quarter of 1863 probing the Mississippi waterways for an alternative route to Vicksburg's back door. The choked and oozy rivers and creeks of Mississippi, however, proved to be very

*For nearly six months, Grant tried to use his hitherto invaluable gunboat flotillas to lodge his army east of Vicksburg's defenses.*

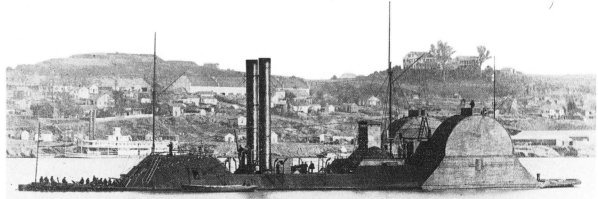

FAR LEFT: *In a desperate hand-to-hand action on the night of July 18, 1863, the Confederate garrison of Battery Wagner on Morris Island hurls back the attacking Union force, thwarting the Northern bid to seal off Charleston by taking the city's coastal forts.*

LEFT: *"Unconditional Surrender" Grant, who, after an unbroken career of victory stretching from Fort Henry to Chattanooga, was appointed* generalissimo *of all Union armies on March 9, 1864.*

different waterways from the Cumberland and Tennessee rivers, which had served Grant so well against Forts Henry and Donelson in February 1862. By the end of March, no less than four attempts to find a way around had failed. Grant now decided that there was nothing for it but to ask Rear Admiral David Porter, commanding the Mississippi ironclad fleet, to run his ships downstream past the Vicksburg batteries. With gunboat support, Grant would then undertake the enormous risk of crossing below the fortress and then, with the Mississippi and Vicksburg itself between him and his base, advance to tackle Pemberton's army.

Grant began the painful southward advance down the Mississippi west bank, from Milliken's Bend to the aptly-named settlement of Hard Times, on March 29. Flooded waterways and wretched going meant that it was April 30 before Grant's army was in position for the crossing. Meanwhile, Porter's gunboats had successfully run the gauntlet of the Vicksburg batteries, braving a spectacular bombardment on the night of April 16. Covered by the US Navy, Grant's army crossed the Mississippi on April 30.

There now followed an amazing seventeen-day campaign in which Grant's achievements surpassed those of

*How Lee's Confederates saw the Union line by the third day at Gettysburg. By singular mischance, the very success of the converging Confederate attacks on the first day had only served to drive Meade's Army into a position of great natural strength.*

204

every successful Union general in the war. Even Lee, or Jackson in his famous Valley Campaign, had never fought a campaign like this. It confounded all the sniping critics who had never ceased to denounce Grant as a liability, a drunkard, a fumbler and a slowpoke, whose occasional flashes of luck did nothing to offset the case for his dismissal. The Vicksburg campaign of May 1–18, 1863, was waged with an initial concentration of 23,000 Union troops against the 50,000-odd under Pemberton's command. Grant's overall achievement was to cancel the disadvantage in numbers by inducing Pemberton to make himself weak everywhere and strong nowhere.

He did this by racing his troops across country, living off the land and "making two days' rations last seven." After two pitched battles at Port Gibson (May 1) and Raymond (May 12), Grant completed his initial sixty-five mile advance from the Mississippi, throwing Joe Johnston out of the city of Jackson and leaving Pemberton isolated to the west. Ably seconded by Sherman, Grant then came back to the west and routed Pemberton's baffled army at Champion's Hill (May 16), twenty miles east of Vicksburg. Johnston got a message through to Pemberton, warning that Vicksburg was now indefensible and that Pemberton should fight his

*The fugitive President. Jefferson Davis doggedly signs the Confederacy's last formal Acts of Government by the roadside, April 1865.*

Successor to Hooker, Burnside and McClellan as commander of the Army of the Potomac — General George G. Meade, the hero of Gettysburg. His victory was all the more remarkable in that he took command of the army on June 27, 1863 — only four days before the first shots were fired at Gettysburg.

The camera records a tense moment at Grant's headquarters. Grant can be seen leaning over Meade's shoulder to consult the map before issuing his orders for the Battle of Cold Harbor, May 21, 1864.

206

Terrified horses lurch through deeply-rutted tracks at Gettysburg. These brave animals played an important role in the war — particularly on the Confederate side, who lost the railroads to the North.

From the "Cyclorama" at Gettysburg, painted by the French artist Philipotteaux after the war: Union guns clatter along the ridge, rushing to shore up a threatened sector of Meade's battle-line.

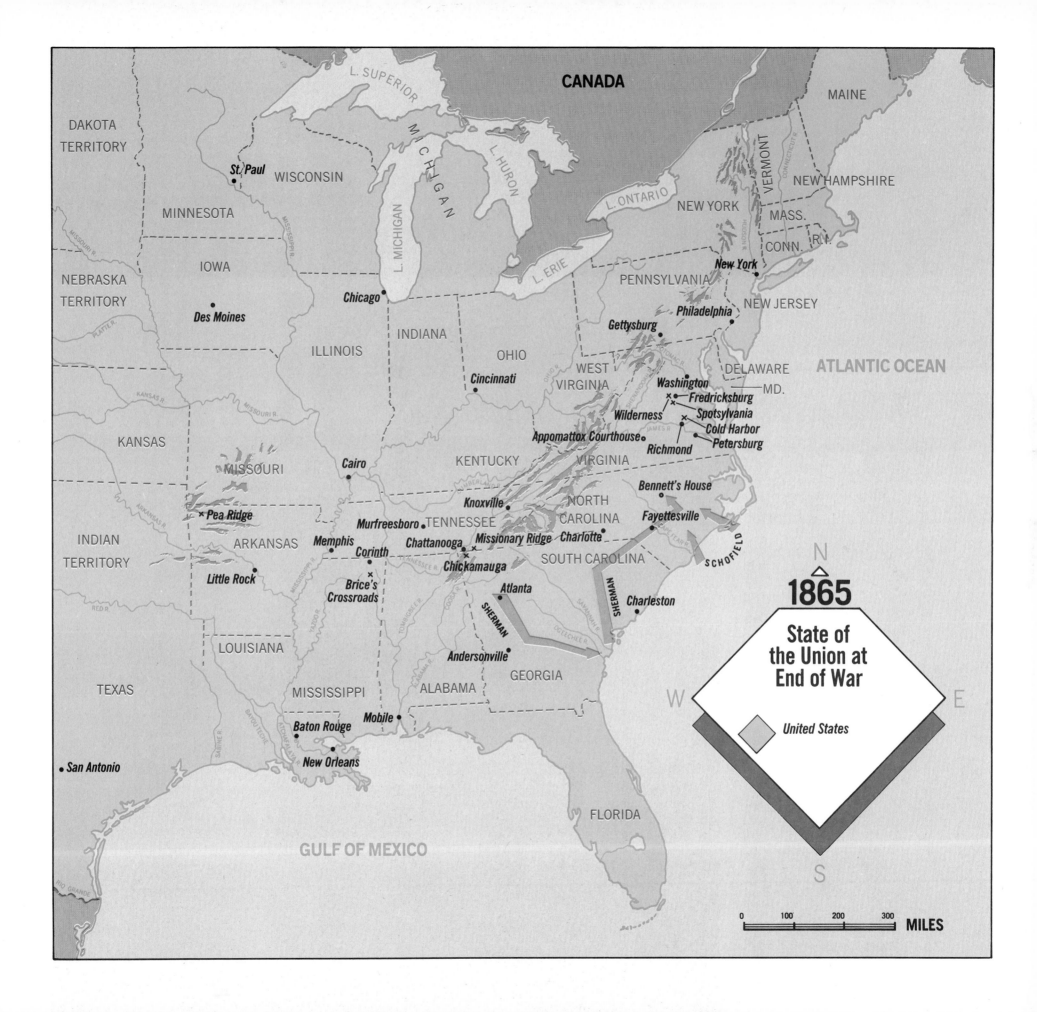

For the first time in the history of warfare, portrait photography was available to the ordinary soldier. But did anyone warn this tough-looking Union infantryman that his stylish white crossbelts made him an easy target in the age of the rifle?

## CERTIFICATE OF HONOR.

Awarded to

of Co. Regt

**FOR BRAVERY AND GOOD CONDUCT,**

**AS A SOLDIER,**

*in the Cause of his Country.*

*A soldier's reward "For Bravery and Good Conduct": a Certificate of Honor, issued by the US Army.*

way out, but Pemberton, fearing piecemeal destruction of his army in open country, withdrew his surviving 31,000 men into the formidable trench defenses of Vicksburg.

### The Siege of Vicksburg

Driving Pemberton into the trenches at Vicksburg was not the result Grant had hoped for. He had wanted to meet Pemberton's army and annihilate it, then walk straight into Vicksburg and end the campaign at a stroke. Now he had to sit down to a formal siege, which began on May 19. After two attempts to batter a path through the Confederate lines by direct assault failed (May 19 and 22), Grant wisely decided against squandering further manpower. Hunger would succeed where the gallantry of Grant's men could not. As June came in, after the first fortnight of siege, the only hope for the

beleaguered citizens and garrison of Vicksburg was that by some miracle Joe Johnston would fight his way through to the city's relief. This could only have been achieved with substantial reinforcements from the Army of Northern Virginia, however, and against this Robert E. Lee had resolutely set his face. Even if Vicksburg was doomed, there was still the chance of exchanging a queen for a queen—avenging Pemberton's lost army by the destruction of the Army of the Potomac, brought to battle on Union soil.

### The Hound at Lee's Heels

When Lee began his march to the Potomac on June 3, his biggest worry was that Hooker would ignore him and go straight for Richmond; but Lee had weighed the odds as accurately as ever. Lincoln's orders to Hooker were precise. Hooker's objective was not Richmond, but

Lee's army; wherever Lee's army went, Hooker was to go—"fret him and fret him." Far from fearing a second invasion of the North, Lincoln positively hoped for one. Nothing else would guarantee a battle with Lee far from his nearest base, and hence—if things went right for once—he would be ripe for destruction.

Things *did* go right for once, and the main reason was the failure of Jeb Stuart, Lee's vital cavalry "eyes" in every previous campaign. On June 9, at Brandy Station, the recently-created cavalry corps of the Army of the Potomac blooded itself in its first clash with Stuart's cavalry. There had never been a full-dress cavalry battle in the Civil War before, largely because the

Confederate cavalry was immeasurably superior; this made Brandy Station an ominous new sensation for Stuart's veteran troopers. Not only were they completely surprised by the Union cavalry under Brigadier Alfred Pleasanton, but they had to fight for their lives. At the end of the day, Pleasanton's cavalry withdrew across the Rappahannock, but the Jeb Stuart legend would never be the same again. For Lee's army, Brandy Station would have fateful results in the weeks ahead.

Lee's main line of march to the Potomac was through the Shenandoah, with Jackson's old corps most ably commanded by Lieutenant-General Richard S. Ewell in the lead. Ewell, a legend in his own right, had lost a leg

*RIGHT: A scene from the Gettysburg Cyclorama: with mere yards separating them, infantrymen shoot wildly at each other.*

*FAR RIGHT: Another detail from the Gettysburg Cyclorama: a battery unlimbered and in action in the center of the Union line.*

A dead Confederate soldier, his rifle artfully propped to make the photograph more poignant, in the rocky fastness of "Devil's Den". This was one of the sectors where the fighting raged fiercest on the second day of Gettysburg.

July 5, 1863: two days after the breaking of Pickett's fatal charge, Confederate dead were still strewn over the Gettysburg Heights. The opening of the battlefield cemetery, immortalized by Lincoln's beautifully-phrased Gettysburg Address, took place on November 19, 1863.

Here, at right, Union
surgeons operate at top speed
in an open-sided shack,
struggling with the
nightmare task of coping
with the flood of Gettysburg
wounded.

These views of Camp Convalescent near Alexandria might have been seen through rose-colored spectacles. The neat formation of troops, the prim hospital, the band and even a library are depicted — with no sign of fleas, dirt, cold, hunger, or the terrors of war.

*The Battle of Chickamauga — September 20, 1863 — was the last Confederate attempt to turn the tide in the West. General Hood is wounded as another Confederate charge breaks on the Union battle-line.*

at Groveton, on the eve of 2nd Bull Run, and was obliged to command his corps from a light carriage. Nonetheless, he hounded his men down the valley in a style that Jackson himself would have envied, crushing a Union force at Winchester under Major-General Robert Milroy. On June 15 Ewell's corps crossed the Potomac, with A. P. Hill and Longstreet bringing up the rear.

## A Confederate Lull Mistimed

All Stuart had to do now was to keep Lee informed of the moment when Hooker set off for the Potomac in pursuit, but this he failed to do. Still seething from the reverses of Brandy Station, Stuart wanted to bring off a grand coup by another dramatic ride clean round the Army of the Potomac, rejoining Lee in Pennsylvania with accurate news of Hooker's movements by June 26 at the latest. But Stuart started late—on June 25, the day that Hooker began to move—and the whole schedule began

to break down from the outset. Stuart had to make a long detour to reach the Potomac, with the result that Lee invaded Pennsylvania blind. Having heard nothing from Stuart, on whom he had learned to rely implicitly, Lee confidently dispersed his corps to replenish themselves from the rich farms of Pennsylvania until Stuart announced the Union approach. The news which Lee was given on the evening of June 28, however, came as a numbing shock. Not only was Hooker's army already across the Potomac, but it was already up at Frederick, Maryland, ideally placed to strike at any of Lee's scattered corps.

The Union army also had a new commander, Lee was told. Hooker was gone, his resignation accepted with alacrity.

On June 27, Major-General George G. Meade, former commander of Hooker's V Corps, had become the fourth general to command the Army of the Potomac. Little

*LEFT: Prison security at Point Lookout. Every visitor to the camp had to apply for and obtain a pass at the Provost Marshal's office.*

*BELOW: Naive depiction of a Union prisoner-of-war camp painted by a Confederate prisoner, John I. Omenhausser, during his incarceration. Its tranquil simplicity belies the appalling conditions endured by the prisoners. (From* True Sketches and Sayings of Rebel Characters in the Point Lookout Prison, Maryland, *in the Museum and Library of Maryland History, Baltimore).*

was known of Meade other than that he had a reputation for dour tenacity and hard fighting. It was Meade who had led Burnside's left-flank attack at Fredericksburg, and who was one of the very few Union generals ever to have taken Stonewall Jackson by surprise. The news that Meade had taken command a mere twenty-four hours before was trivial, compared with the danger which his approach represented to the Army of Northern Virginia. Lee immediately ordered his corps commanders—Ewell, A. P. Hill, and Longstreet—to concentrate at the nearest convenient road center. This was a small Pennsylvanian town where no less than eight roads met, three of them being the roads which the Confederate corps must use: the town of Gettysburg.

## Lee vs. Meade: Decision at Gettysburg

Meade meanwhile was advancing into Pennsylvania with the idea of getting between Lee and the cities of Washington and Baltimore, while also stopping Lee from crossing the Susquehanna River and making for Philadelphia. When his scouts told him that Ewell was pulling back from Carlisle—the furthest north reached by the Army of Northern Virginia—Meade decided to concentrate at Pipe Creek, fifteen miles south of Gettysburg. Up to the north, in Gettysburg, Meade already had a cavalry screen of three brigades under Major-General John Buford. To guard against any surprise from the north, Meade sent Major-General John F. Reynolds to join Buford at Gettysburg.

*FAR LEFT: The storming of Missionary Ridge — November 25, 1863 — by Grant's Army of the Cumberland. This assault through Bragg's blockading army broke the Confederate hold on Chattanooga for good, opening the road into Georgia.*

*BELOW: Conditions for prisoners-of-war were horrendous. Here David Gilmour Blythe shows the Confederate "Libby Prison".*

If all had gone according to the plans of Lee and Meade, the two armies would have concentrated on July 1—the Confederates at Gettysburg, the Unionists at Pipe Creek. A day or so of cautious probing would have ensued, followed by a battle for which both armies would have been fully prepared. The actual Battle of Gettysburg was entirely different. Just for once, the troops started the battle before their generals were ready. The units in first contact had no orders to do what they did. They merely obeyed an instinct to fight, and the resultant escalation of the encounter produced the three-day Battle of Gettysburg (July 1–3, 1863).

On the morning of the first day, A. P. Hill's leading division approached Gettysburg from the west, and ran straight into Buford's cavalry. As a good cavalryman, Buford should have fallen back to notify Meade of Lee's advance, but instead he decided to fight a dismounted action in defence of the town. His dismounted troopers were being steadily pushed back when Reynolds arrived from the south, and also decided that Gettysburg must be held. Reynolds led his corps forward to check Hill and was shot dead at the first clash. Ewell's corps came down from the north just as Major-General Oliver O. Howard's XI Corps came up from the south. And so the battle swelled, with the corps of Reynolds and Howard forming a loose arc north of the town, an arc which was steadily pushed inwards by the converging attacks of Hill and Ewell. By mid-afternoon on July 1, the Unionists had been pushed out of Gettysburg, instinctively falling back to take the knolls and ridges of the high ground south of the town, which included Cemetery Hill, Culp's Hill, and the north–south length of Cemetery Ridge.

Riding to the scene, Lee and Meade were left to make the best of it. Meade's task was by far the easier; his forces had been pushed back into a position of promising strength, with the Army of the Potomac holding all the high ground. He would fight where he stood, letting Lee come to him. Lee could see few opportunities to use his favorite tactics. Hill and Ewell had presented him with

the initiative, but it left him with little alternative other than to try to batter Meade's divisions out of their positions. Above all, Lee did not have Stuart to provide accurate information about the enemy's flanks and most dangerous reserves. It was not until July 2 that Stuart actually rejoined Lee with his exhausted cavalry brigades—far too late to be of any use.

The second day of Gettysburg saw Confederate attacks hammering the southern end of Meade's line, taking the Peach Orchard and the Wheat Field but failing before the rocky tangles of Devil's Den and the stoutly-held crests of Little Round Top and Big Round Top. By nightfall on the 2nd, Lee had evolved the only strategy which seemed likely to work. After subjecting Meade's center to a concentrated artillery bombardment, he would send in his last three fresh divisions—Pickett, Pettigrew, and Trimble—cutting the Army of the Potomac in two. This would be the master-stroke; if it failed, there would be precious little else that Lee could do.

*The storming of Missionary Ridge.*

## The Greatest American Battle

The morning of July 3, the third day, was taken up with assembling the Confederate artillery for the great bombardment. This was in fact the heaviest bombardment ever seen on the North American continent: 130 guns, ranged nearly wheel to wheel. When their fire crashed out at about 1.00pm and the Union guns replied from Cemetery Ridge, the result was over 200 guns firing at once, within the area of a single square mile. Even this torrent of shot and shell failed to sweep the long blue lines from Cemetery Ridge. They were still there when the Confederate drumfire tapered off shortly after 3.00pm, and the three Confederate divisions rolled forward to the attack.

"Pickett's Charge," as it will always be remembered, was only one of many such acts of supreme gallantry in the American Civil War; yet, more than most, it was to achieve a kind of immortality, ranking beside the repulse of the Old Guard at Waterloo, the Charge of the

*ABOVE: Stirring depiction of Grant's assault on the Confederate trench lines defending Vicksburg, which took place on May 19, 1863. In fact the Union attack was repulsed with heavy losses, and Grant was forced to tighten the siege and wait for hunger to compel surrender.*

*FAR LEFT: Another of Winslow Homer's masterpieces captures the pathos of the prisoner — a sullen trio of Confederate captives, their wide range of ages reflecting the Confederacy's enduring problems of insufficient manpower.*

*Even after capture and consignment to a prison camp, the war went on — this time against "graybacks", or lice. These are Confederate prisoners, pursuing the enemy in the Point Lookout camp, Maryland.*

*The battlefield of Lookout Mountain (center) where Grant's troops finally broke the Confederate hold on Chattanooga in November 1863.*

Light Brigade at Balaclava, or the equally-doomed onslaught of the Prussian Guard at First Ypres in 1914. Here were 15,000 men, the pick of Lee's army, sweeping forward in close formation under a murderous fire, yet never wavering. Only a few hundred managed to break into the Union line, led by the gallant Brigadier Lewis Armistead, who fell dead with his hand on a Union gun. And then, suddenly, the survivors were coming back— half of them. The task undertaken by Pickett's Charge had been beyond human courage, and with it died Lee's last hope of victory at Gettysburg.

It was not the first time that two armies had fought each other to a standstill. Nearly 50,000 Americans fell at Gettysburg: some 25,000 Union troops, 21,000 Confederates. When Lee retreated on July 4, it was with a wagon-train of wounded seventeen miles long. Meade, overwhelmed by his victory, was more than glad to see him go. Lincoln was incensed by Meade's failure to follow up the victory, especially as Lee's pontoon bridge over the Potomac had been partially destroyed. But Meade's leading columns did not appear until July 12, and Lee recrossed the Potomac for the last time on the

*Near the end: desperate Confederate citizens of besieged Vicksburg, caught in the open and panicked by plunging Union shellfire.*

night of the 13th. Lee's supreme effort, the last Confederate invasion of the North, was over. As Winston Churchill was later to write: "He had lost only two guns, and the war."

### The Mississippi Falls to the North

Northern exultation at the victory of Gettysburg was heightened by electrifying news from the West. On July 4—Independence Day—General Pemberton surrendered Vicksburg to Grant after an exhausting six-and-a-half week siege. Four days later, 150 miles downstream from the surrendered fortress whose trenches had never been broken, Port Hudson surrendered in its turn. At long last, the entire length of the Mississippi River lay under Union control.

Port Hudson fell to Major-General Nathaniel P. Banks, unlucky veteran of the Valley Campaign, of whom Jackson had once commented "He is always ready to fight and generally gets whipped." Banks certainly did not represent the best military brains of the United States Army, but he knew well enough what the fall of Port Hudson meant to the Confederates. As he wrote to his wife: "We have taken from them the power to establish an independent government. It can never be done between the Mississippi and the Atlantic. You can tell your friends that the Confederacy is an impossibility."

So, indeed, it was—but another twenty-one months of bloody conflict would pass before that impossibility would finally be accepted.

# 10 Victory of the Union: 1864 - 1865

THE LONG MISSISSIPPI CAMPAIGN was over, with the result that Texas, Arkansas and Louisiana had been severed from the body of the Confederacy. Lee's battle-worn survivors had completed their retreat to northern Virginia. And now, in the autumn of 1863, there remained only one sector where the Confederacy could strike back at its oncoming foes. This was on the border of Tennessee and Georgia, where the last intact Confederate Army in the West represented the only surviving obstacle to a Union invasion of the Deep South.

Six months after its mauling at Murfreesboro, Rosecrans' army finally resumed its cautious advance on Chattanooga. This time there were to be no risks, and Rosecrans took all the time he needed to maneuver Braxton Bragg out of Chattanooga without a fight. On September 4, Chattanooga fell painlessly into Rosecrans' hands, but nemesis was about to strike him from the East.

## The War in the Western South

During the late summer of 1863, in the bitter aftermath of Gettysburg and Vicksburg, the choice facing Jefferson Davis was stark. Bragg could not retreat indefinitely; there was nowhere for him to stand between the southern Tennessee state line and Atlanta,

*FAR LEFT: From Atlanta to the sea; the agony of the doomed Confederacy begins in earnest with Sherman's punitive march through Georgia, 1864.*

*BELOW: Grant on the eve of the dreadful Wilderness campaign in which the Union general pinned his hopes on the murderous process of attrition.*

Georgia. Davis therefore steeled himself to the decision which he had declined to make on Pemberton's behalf back in May and June. He would send powerful reinforcements west by rail and he would obtain these reinforcements from the Army of Northern Virginia. By the time the decision had been made, after prolonged haggling with Lee, the Confederacy's ability to send these reinforcements efficiently had been severely impeded. In the last week of August, Burnside had advanced south across Kentucky into Tennessee, occupying Knoxville and thus cutting one of the last crucial Confederate rail links. When reinforcements (Longstreet's corps), began to entrain on September 9, they faced a painful 500-mile rail detour before they could reach Bragg on September 18. By this time, Rosecrans had begun to sense that Bragg was considering the possibility of a counter-offensive. He concentrated his army near West Chickamauga Creek, some ten miles south of Chattanooga, in the nick of time to receive the onslaught which broke on him on September 20, 1863.

## Chickamauga: End of an Era

The Battle of Chickamauga marked the end of an era, repeating for the last time the gory pattern set at Shiloh and Murfreesboro. It was the last Confederate attack in the West and, as ever, a partial success would not be enough. The stakes were infinite: Bragg was expected not merely to destroy Rosecrans and recover Chattanooga, but to sweep on and recover the whole of Tennessee. In the event, it was the old story. The Confederate attack broke the Union right flank and drove

*FAR LEFT: January 1864: Grant's army grimly edges closer to the prize of Vicksburg in a hard-fought clash at Jacksonville, Mississippi.*

*BELOW: The punishment of Atlanta begins: ripping up the railroad tracks after the city's fall, September 1864.*

PREVIOUS PAGE: *Spotsylvania Courthouse, one of the worst death-struggles between Lee and Grant in the 1864 fighting, in which yet again the virtue of a well-conceived trench system was bloodily displayed. Grant was left with no alternative but to disengage, feeling in vain for the open flank which Lee refused to offer him.*

RIGHT: *This is Major Albert G. Enos, of the 8th Pennsylvanian Cavalry Regiment.*

LEFT: *Major-General Potter and his staff prepare for battle in the gloomy woods of the Wilderness, May 1864.*

BELOW: *A Confederate muzzle-loader peers through a sand-bagged gun embrasure in the Atlanta siege lines.*

exultantly forward, only to be stopped dead by the improvised Union defense lines wrapped hastily around Snodgrass Hill by General "Pap" Thomas—"The Rock of Chickamauga." Rosecrans accompanied his beaten men back to Chattanooga; Thomas followed with his unbeaten corps on the 21st, and once again Bragg was denied the fruits of victory by his very success. Once again, wickedly heavy losses (16,000 Union, over 20,000 Confederate) left neither army capable of immediate action. The last great Confederate effort in the West had failed.

**The Tide Turns for the Union**
The burden was now passed to Grant, who on October 16, 1863, was appointed overall commander of the Armies of the Ohio, Cumberland, and the Tennessee rivers. Rosecrans, dismissed from the command of the Army of the Tennessee, was replaced by Grant's lieutenant, Sherman. Taking personal command at Chattanooga, Grant's immediate task was to clear Bragg's army off the arc of hills looking down on the city. He planned to win with converging attacks by

*ABOVE: End of the line for the Confederate raider CSS* Alabama, *sunk off Cherbourg by the USS* Kearsarge *on June 19, 1864, after a remarkable two-year cruise in which she accounted for 20 Union ships.*

*FAR LEFT: At Cold Harbor in June 1864 — on the old Seven Days battlefield of 1862 — Lee managed yet again to fight Grant to a standstill, with nearly 7,000 Union troops falling in less than an hour. After this new setback Grant took the audacious decision to break clean away and shift his line of attack from the northern approaches to Richmond to the southern.*

"Fighting Joe" Hooker against Lookout Mountain, and Sherman against the extremity of Missionary Ridge. The terrain in front of Sherman proved impassable, and the attack seemed to be foundering, whereupon Thomas's watching ranks in the Union center swarmed forward in an attack which Grant had not ordered, and which conjured up horrifying memories of Pickett's Charge. Under Grant's helpless eyes, however, Thomas's men swept Missionary Ridge and broke the South's tenuous hold on Chattanooga for good. The road into Georgia lay open.

The storming of Missionary Ridge closed a momentous year for the Union. It had opened in the despondent aftermath of Fredericksburg, Chickasaw Bluff, and Murfreesboro, with the Confederacy's capacity for resistance apparently unbroken; by the end of the year, the Confederates had been cleared from the Mississippi, chased out of Tennessee, and faced relentless attrition in Virginia. And now, for the first time since the war had begun, a winter lull descended on the conflict. Down to its last meager resources, the Confederacy had no hope of regaining the initiative, and neither Lincoln nor his generals saw any reason to throw away their advantages on the hazard of premature action.

## Grant: Supreme Commander, 1864

When the armies moved again in spring 1864, Lincoln had taken another momentous decision. He became the first wartime President to entrust the military operations of the Union to a single supreme commander: Grant, who was appointed Commander-in-Chief of the Armies of the United States on March 9, 1864. Appointing Sherman to command in Georgia, Grant now headed East to his first encounter with Robert E. Lee.

Grant had achieved wonders during his Western campaigns; but now, in Virginia, the bloody spring and summer of 1864 had a brutal lesson to teach—one which

this war was fated to bequeath forgotten to the warring nations of Europe in 1914. This was the terrible effect of massed firepower against troops attacking in close order, and the frustrating strength of well-sited trench defenses. Grant's first trial of strength with Lee was made between May 5–12, 1864, in the double Battle of the Wilderness and of Spotsylvania Court House. The Wilderness was the dreary stretch of woodland through which Stonewall Jackson had advanced, twelve months before, to rout Hooker's right flank at Chancellorsville. There, on May 5–6, 1864, Grant attacked Lee with 120,000 men against 60,000.

*FAR LEFT: The victory that sealed the fate of Atlanta: Hood's assault on the Union at Jonesboro, Georgia was broken on September 1, 1864, leaving the Confederates no choice but to evacuate the city.*

*FAR LEFT, BOTTOM: William Tecumseh Sherman, hand on hip, in the Atlanta siege lines, July 1864.*

*BELOW: Accepting the end. With less than two days of freedom left to him, Jefferson Davis bids his last escort farewell.*

*Cedar Creek, October 19, 1864: Sheridan's charge recoups the damage done by Early's surprise attack – a storming counter-stroke which routed Early's men and earned Sheridan promotion to the rank of major-general.*

In two days of appalling fighting Grant was fought to a standstill, but he did not give up. He slipped past Lee's right flank, Lee countered, and the killing was resumed before the Confederate rifle-pits covering Spotsylvania. The slaughter lasted from May 8 to May 19 and cost Grant another 18,000 casualties.

Still Grant would not give up. He slipped to the left yet again, with Lee keeping pace for dear life, and by the end of May the two armies had reached the old battle-field of the Seven Days. At Cold Harbor (June 1–3) Grant attacked again. This time he had to acknowledge that the day of the frontal assault was over, when the Army of the Potomac suffered nearly 7,000 losses in a single hour.

It was now that Grant demonstrated the genius behind the brutal policy of "attrition" which he had promised Lee. He changed his whole plan, disengaged, and shipped nearly the whole of his army down to the James, where Beauregard was already holding Butler in check at Bermuda Hundred. Grant had marked down the rail junction of Petersburg as the southern key to Richmond, but by June 18, after a start of fleeting promise, the latest Union move ground to a halt in front of the deepening Confederate trenches screening Petersburg. In a month and a half of combat, the like of which the world had never seen before, Lee had succeeded in saving Richmond yet again. But the Army of Northern Virginia was now committed to trench warfare. For the rest of the year it was stalemate, although the life of Lee's army was now measured by the length of time it could manage to hang on, dug in at Petersburg.

*FAR LEFT: The last of the Confederate Gulf seaports passes under Union control. Perched in the rigging of his flagship* Hartford, *Admiral Farragut directs the Battle of Mobile Bay (August 5, 1864).*

*BELOW: The Union's vengeance, as the conspirators who planned Lincoln's murder are prepared for execution.*

*Final tailpiece of the long Tennessee campaign: the Battle of Nashville (December 15, 1864). Hood's last Confederate foray into Tennessee was driven back into Mississippi, never to return.*

FAR LEFT: *Lincoln's successor: Vice-President Andrew Johnson, photographed shortly before his shock accession to the Presidency.*

LEFT: *One of the most famous Matthew Brady photographs of the last year of the war—the tedium of prolonged trench warfare, captured by this shot of Union troops before Petersburg in 1864.*

## Sherman's March Through Atlanta to the Sea

While Lee and Grant engaged in this horrific death-struggle before Richmond, Sherman was beginning his march on Atlanta. Sherman's Georgia campaign of 1864 fell into four phases: from May 5 to July 17, while he fenced Joe Johnston back and back to the outskirts of Atlanta; from July 17—when Johnston was dismissed and replaced by Major-General John B. Hood—to September 1, when Hood finally abandoned Atlanta; from September 1 to November 15, when Sherman finally left Hood to his own devices; and finally from November 15 to December 22. The latter phase was the most famous (or notorious); the "March to the Sea," in which Sherman cut loose from all communications and traced a blackened, burning scar across the face of Georgia, finally emerging on the coast to capture Savannah. In this extraordinary campaign, the actual capture of Atlanta was incidental. Sherman demonstrated his

*FAR LEFT: Five Forks, April 1, 1865 — Sheridan's assault smashes through the totally surprised Confederate lines, and at long last the Confederate grip on the Petersburg siege lines is broken.*

*BELOW: Risking the assassination which was to reach him in his own capital only ten days later, Abraham Lincoln visits captured Richmond on April 4, 1865 without an escort, his path thronged with exultant former slaves crying "Glory, glory!".*

**247**

*The fast-moving General Philip Sheridan, whose seizure of Appomattox Station blocked Lee's escape route and left the Confederate commander with no option but to surrender.*

formidable evolution as a thinking general—he had come a long way from his pessimistic days in Kentucky—when he suddenly realized that he need no longer concentrate on the militarily correct objective of Hood's army. By taking the bulk of his army across Georgia to the sea, he would be admirably placed for a decisive campaign in 1865. This would enable him to strike north through the Carolinas, pushing the last army of the confederacy closer and closer to the Virginia theater. With its promise of an early end to the war, Sherman's capture of Savannah was indeed a timely Christmas present for President Lincoln, who had been re-elected in November 1864.

## The Last Act: Richmond Abandoned

The last act began, ironically enough, when Jefferson Davis appointed Lee General-in-Chief of the Con-federate Armies in February 1865. The wheel had nearly come full circle for that incomparable commander, who had been offered the same position in the Army of the United States before Virginia's secession in 1861. One of the greatest ifs of the American Civil War is to ponder the course the war might have taken had Davis only taken this step two years before. As it was, in February 1865, Lee could do little more than im-mediately restore Johnston as commander of the southern army. Lee also suggested that his own army should break out of the trap which Grant was building for it at Petersburg, and drive south to join hands with Johnston. United, the last two armies of the Con-federacy would have at least a chance of defeating Sherman, destroying the southern jaw of the closing Union pincers. But Davis refused; the last act was to be fought out at Petersburg and Richmond.

*The Confederate capital falls at last, after nearly four years of war: the night sky over burning Richmond, April 2–3, 1865.*

*South side of R.R. workshop—*

*Bridge on the Appomattox — Train of Cars and Workshop A.R.W.*

Thus came the last battle. It opened on March 31 with Sheridan's capture of the Five Forks strongpoint—lost by Pickett, of Gettysburg fame, with the accompanying calamity of the death of A. P. Hill. Lee advised Davis to evacuate Richmond, which was done on Sunday, April 2, 1865; Lee himself then broke out to the west. He planned to join hands with Ewell and whatever troops had been saved from Richmond, then head south down the Richmond & Danville Railroad in the direction of Johnston's army. Unluckily for him, this escape route was closed by Sheridan on April 5, leaving no option but another wide detour to the west along the line of the Appomattox River, away from Johnston. Sheridan, scenting victory, cabled "If the thing is pressed I think Lee will surrender"; to which Lincoln replied, "Let the thing be pressed." Forty-eight hours later, with less than 8,000 effective troops under his command, Lee heard that Sheridan had beaten him to Appomattox Court House and was now squarely in his path. It was enough. Lee promptly sent a flag of truce to Grant, announcing his willingness to discuss the surrender terms which he had rejected on the 7th.

### The Final Curtain: Appomattox

At Appomattox on April 9, 1865, Lee surrendered all that was left of the Army of Northern Virginia—8,000 passable soldiers and 15,000 ragged, starving teenagers and boys. Lee's unshakeable dignity throughout the surrender proceedings went into Confederate legend, but it was assisted by the generosity of the terms offered by Grant. Lee's surrendered men must keep their horses, Grant gently insisted; they would be needed for the spring plowing.

The last act of madness occurred on the night of April 14, when Abraham Lincoln was assassinated in his box at Ford's Theater. The Derringer bullet fired by John Wilkes Booth did nothing to prolong the hopeless struggle, for Joe Johnston surrendered to Sherman as soon as he heard of Lee's capitulation. Negotiations began at Durham Station, North Carolina, on April 17, and were concluded on April 26, when Johnston formally surrendered to Sherman, accepting the terms to which Lee had agreed at Appomattox. Jefferson Davis, a disguised fugitive, was captured by Union cavalry near Irwinsville, Georgia, on May 10. The last shots of the war were fired at Palmito Ranch, Texas, on the Rio Grande on May 13, 1865, and General Kirby Smith, commanding the already non-existent Confederate forces west of the Mississippi, made the last surrender to the power of Union arms on May 26. Four years and one month since the first shell had burst over Fort Sumter, the American Civil War was over.

*The stuff of legend . . .*

## Prominent Confederate and Union Generals and Statesmen of the Civil War

### STATESMEN

1. Cameron
2. Stanton
3. Chase
4. Seward
5. Lincoln
6. Davis
7. Stephens
8. Benjamin
9. Toombs
10. Yancey

### GENERALS

| | |
|---|---|
| 11. Van Dorn | 31. Hancock |
| 12. A.S. Johnston | 32. Sheridan |
| 13. Ewell | 33. Howard |
| 14. Price | 34. Burnside |
| 15. Hood | 35. Sigel |
| 16. Stuart | 36. Rosencrans |
| 17. Bragg | 37. Sherman |
| 18. Buckner | 38. Thomas |
| 19. Breckinridge | 39. Grant |
| 20. Pemberton | 40. Meade |
| 21. Kearney | 41. J.E. Johnston |
| 22. Blair | 42. Lee |
| 23. Stoneman | 43. Beauregard |
| 24. Slocum | 44. Longstreet |
| 25. McPherson | 45. Hampton |
| 26. Logan | 46. Hill |
| 27. Sickles | 47. Forrest |
| 28. Pope | 48. Jackson |
| 29. McClellan | 49. Polk |
| 30. Hooker | 50. Morgan |

ABOVE: *Under the white flag, Robert E. Lee is conducted through the Union lines to his meeting with U.S. Grant at Appomattox.*

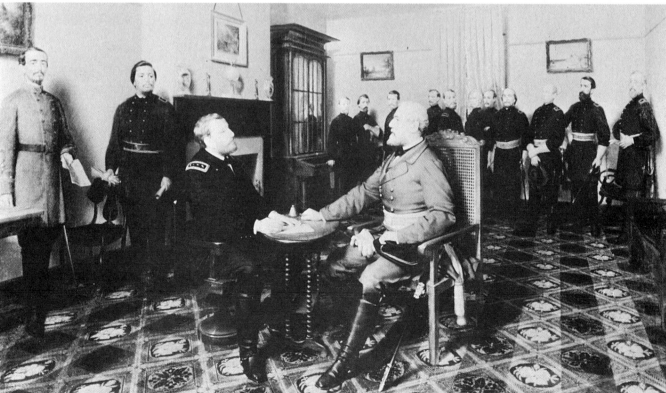

RIGHT: *Greatness in defeat. Lee accepts Grant's terms at Appomattox Court House. Those terms were generous: no "unconditional surrender", or humiliating parades of defeated troops, but a straightforward disarming of Lee's men followed by their return home on parole.*

ABOVE: *The man on the white horse; mounted on the ever-faithful "Traveler", Robert E.Lee rides away from the scene of his surrender. To his men, Lee announced: "With an increasing admiration of your constancy and devotion to your country, and a grateful remembrance of your kind and generous consideration for myself, I bid you all an affectionate farewell".*

LEFT: *Grim symptom of a conflict which had become an all-out war by the summer of 1864: a refugee Southern family takes to the road.*

RIGHT: *The mad, meaningless deed which removed the one man who could have brought a peace of reconciliation to the defeated South: John Wilkes Booth assassinates Lincoln at Ford's Theater, April 14, 1865.*

BELOW: *The funeral cortège of Abraham Lincoln parades through mourning crowds in Washington.*

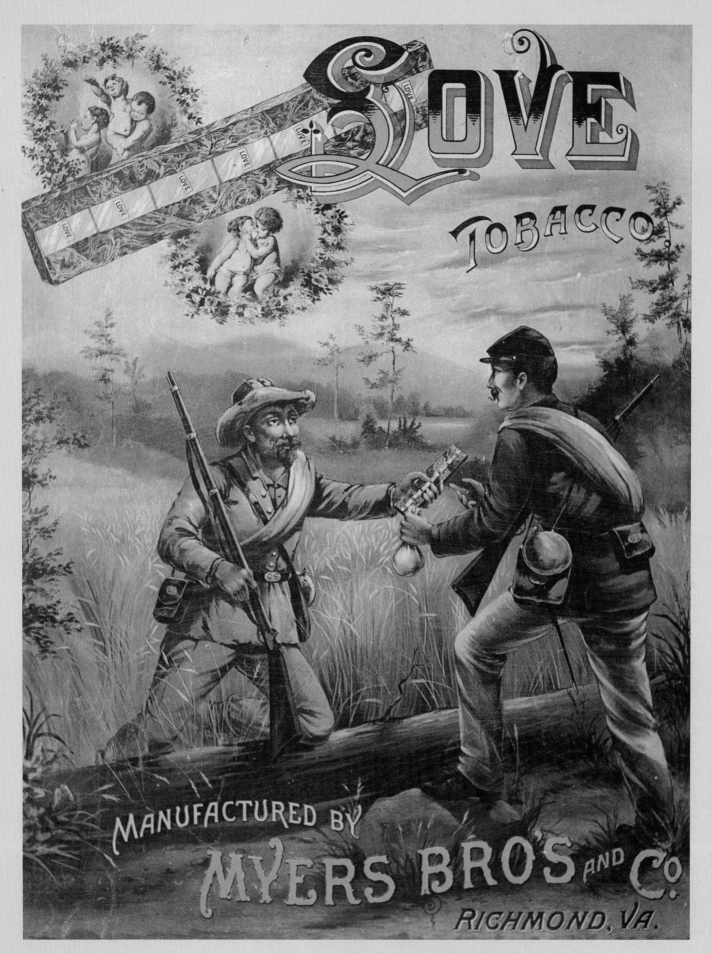

LOVE TOBACCO

MANUFACTURED BY MYERS BROS AND CO. RICHMOND, VA.

*LEFT: Swords into ploughshares: this poster of 1867 wishfully evokes the spirit of reconciliation for which the battle-torn American nation yearned. But in the South the legend of the "Lost Cause" would outlast the bitterness of defeat.*

*OVERLEAF, LEFT: Turning a matchless war record into hard cash. Ex-President Grant, politically discredited and bankrupt, and dying of throat cancer, works on his memoirs to pay off his debts and provide for his family. It was his last battle — and last victory. Grant's memoirs netted his family some $450,000 after his death in 1885.*

*OVERLEAF, RIGHT: Defenses that failed: a vicious-looking spiked chevaux-de-frise obstacle in the Atlanta trenches.*

EXTREME FAR LEFT: This statue bears the inscription: "Love makes memory eternal", and was erected in 1902 in front of the Albemarle County Courthouse in Charlottesville. It is dedicated to the heroism of the Confederate soldiers of Charlottesville, and Albemarle County.

FAR LEFT: Leader of the Lost Cause: the statue of Jefferson Davis at the Vicksburg Battlefield National Park.

LEFT, TOP: The Antietam battlefield cemetery today. The battle still retains a horrifying significance in American history. No other battle of the war produced so many American casualties — 11,172 Union, 12,410 Confederates. Though McClellan failed to destroy the Army of Northern Virginia, Lee had no choice after the battle but to order a withdrawal across the Potomac into Virginia.

LEFT, BELOW: Where one of the most enduring Confederate legends was born, as General Lee yelled "Look! There stands Jackson like a stone wall! Rally behind the Virginians!" Jackson always insisted that his famous nickname properly belonged to his men of the 1st Virginia Brigade — but his statue still stands on the Bull Run battlefield.

# INDEX

Note: Numbers in *italics* refer to pictures

# Picture Credits

**Aldus Archives** 9 16 29 40 44 65 134-135 136 bottom 157 161 187 188 201 208 258 259; **Bridgeman Art Library** "Cotton Exchange" by Degas 14-15; **BBC Hulton Picture Library** 247; **Corina Dvorak** 148 189; **Mary Evans Picture Library** 13 left; **Image Bank** 34 260 261 bottom 265; **MacClancy Collection** Title page 18-19 33 35 bottom 37 40 top 41 42 44 top 52 53 54-55 57 bottom 60 61 64 69 77 78 79 80 81 82 83 84 85 89 92 93 96 97 104-5 108 109 110-111 112 113 121 129 132 136 top 144 148 top 152 153 156 157 top 163 164 172 bottom 173 175 177 180 bottom 184 185 197 199 200 204 205 bottom 212 216 225 229 233 bottom 237 255 bottom 256; **Mansell** 18 21; **Maryland Historical Society** 217 224; **Metropolitan Museum of Art,** gift of Mrs William F. Milton 1923, painting by Winslow Homer 182-183; **Metropolitan Museum of Art,** gift of Mrs Frank B. Porter, painting by Winslow Homer 222-223; **Museum of Fine Arts, Boston,** painting by David Gilmour Blythe 219; **National Park Services** 119 120 152 inset 260 261; **Peter Newark's Western Americana** 6-7 8 10-11 12 15 17 21-23 27 31 39 43 47 49 57 top 58-59 72 74 75 86 87 95 98-99 106-107 114-115 122-123 126-127 130-131 138-139 158 159 162 170 171 178 179 196 198-199 206 210 211 213 226 227 232 235 240-241 244-245 248 249 254 bottom 255 top; **The Virginia Historical Society,** Battle Abbey Murals 146-147.
All other images courtesy of Library of Congress/Multimedia Publications.

**Cartography by Matthew Ward.**

**Multimedia Books Limited have endeavored to observe the legal requirements with regard to the suppliers of photographic material.**